DEVELOPING APACHE SPARK APPLICATIONS WITH PYTHON

NEREO CAMPOS & XAVIER MORERA

Cover designed by Sol Vega

This book is a work of fiction. Names, characters, places, and incidents either are products of the author's imagination or are used fictitiously. Any resemblance to actual persons, living or dead, events, or locales is entirely coincidental.

Xavier Morera
Visit my website at www.xaviermorera.com

Printed in the United States of America

First Printing: Dec 2019
Big Data Inc

ISBN-13: 978-1-6764141-5-5

CONTENTS

Xavier

To my wife and kids:

   Irenita, Juli, and Luci for their patience with my crazy dream of being an entrepreneur and author instead of an employee.

ACKNOWLEDGMENTS

XAVIER: I want to thank my wife for her extreme patience during my long days sitting at a computer, and with my crazy dream of being an entrepreneur and author instead of an employee. This includes my daughters whom I love so much, Juli and Luci. One day you will understand why I spend so much time in the "ficina". Also to my grandparents; Tito taught me the value of hard work and honesty, and Tata gave me the idea of working on building my dream instead of being hired to help someone else build theirs. My mother and father too; they are exemplary human beings.

There are other people who have helped me in my life; you know who you are. Maynor, will it scale? Kamran, I'll tell you what I am working on right now. Tom, you are secretly my mentor, both on Georgia food, Linux stuff, and content creation. Jim, give me a hug! Beth, who is your favorite? Mike W., I'll never forget the story arc. Simon A., I promise I'll get to live video soon. Jason, how do the numbers look... and build another course! Ramon, everyone should have a friend like you. Rolo, we have enough cars. Boby, get a daily driver. Adrian, thanks for the office and the VR. Dani, how do you do it? Brad, we have to go climb a mountain or have a beer.

Thanks to Elisa and team for proofreading the book, and Peter for the technical review. You both rock.

Sol, great work on getting the book ready for publishing and for all the editing that you've done. Wonderful work!

And of course, the main guy in this book. The person that you look to when you have a technical problem to solve... Nereo. He is a human table of contents for anything technology-related. He makes things look so easy, when they are not.

So many more, but those are some that I want to mention by name

NEREO: I would like to thank my family.

Xavier Morera & Nereo Campos

1 The Spark Era

Ever since the dawn of civilization, humans have had a need for organizing data. Accounting has existed for thousands of years. It was initially used to account for crops and herds, but later on was adopted for many other uses. Simple analog methods were used at first, which at some point evolved into mechanical devices.

Fast-forward a few years, and we get to the digital era, where things like databases and spreadsheets started to be used to manage ever-growing amounts of data. How much data? A lot. More than what a human could manage in their mind or using analog methods, and it's still growing.

Paraphrasing a smart man, developing applications that worked with data went something like this: You took a group of developers, put them into a room, fed them a lot of pizza, and wrote a big check for the largest database that you could buy, and another one for the largest metal box on the market. Eventually, you got an application capable of handling large amounts of data for your enterprise. But as expected, things change—they always do, don't they?

We reached an era of information explosion, in large part thanks to the internet. Data started to be created at an unprecedented rate; so much so that some of these data sets cannot be managed and processed using traditional methods.

In fact, we can say that the internet is partly responsible for taking us into the Big Data era. Hadoop was created at Yahoo to help crawl the internet, something that could not be done with traditional methods. The Yahoo engineers that created Hadoop were inspired by two papers released by Google that explained how they solved the problem of working with large amounts of data in parallel.

But Big Data was more than just Hadoop. Soon enough, Hadoop, which initially was meant to refer to the framework used for distributed processing of large amounts of data (MapReduce), started to become more of an umbrella term to describe an ecosystem of tools and platforms capable of massive parallel processing of data. This included Pig, Hive, Impala, and many more.

But sometime around 2009, a research project in UC Berkeley AMPLab was started by Matei Zaharia. At first, according to legend, the original project was building a cluster management framework, known as mesos. Once mesos was born, they wanted to see how easy it was to build a framework from scratch in mesos, and that's how Spark was born.

They open-sourced the code in 2010, donating it to the Apache Foundation in 2013, with it becoming a top-level project in 2014. It has grown both in terms of company usage and number of contributors, which is over 1400at this time.

Spark is fast, and it integrates with many different platforms and storage platforms. It can be used for data engineering or machine learning. Knowledge of Apache Spark is an excellent skill to have in your toolbelt. Let's get started—welcome to the Spark era!

2 Understanding Apache Spark

If you are reading this book, it's because you have a pretty good idea of what Spark is, or at least what it is used for. There are millions of applications that could benefit from the programming model proposed by Spark; there is tons of data waiting to be analyzed to bring to life powerful insights that can change the course of a business. Perhaps you have seen the very catching and powerful phrase from Apache Spark's site, "lightning-fast unified analytics engine." What does this really mean? Can Spark solve all problems? What is Apache Spark? How does it work? In this chapter, we will show you features of Spark that make it amazing.

Spark is an open source cluster computing framework intended to be used in processing and analyzing large amounts of data, just like Hadoop MapReduce but better. Processing of batch and streaming data has a huge impact because Spark achieves high performance, and it scales really well. Apart from the high performance achieved by Spark, there are other benefits that make it powerful and easy to use.

Spark redefines the way we work with Big Data as an open source, lightning-fast, general purpose and distributed framework that is easy to use and easy to learn, with a large and vibrant community, and that operates very well with the rest of the Hadoop ecosystem as well as other platforms, products and cloud services.

As a firm believer that there is no better way to learn than with an example, let's start diving into the Spark ecosystem with one. We are going to use a data dump from Stack Overflow's posts, which can be found in **https://archive.org/download/stackexchange**.

Let's imagine that you are part of a team that is using National Oceanic and Atmospheric Association (NOAA) data for analysis. This is an extract of the two datasets:

STATION	DATE	OBSERVATION	VALUE	MF	QF	SF	TIME
US1MISW005	20180101	PRCP	0	null	null	N	null
US1MISW005	20180101	SNOW	0	null	null	N	null
CA1MB000296	20180101	PRCP	0	null	null	N	null
ASN00015643	20180101	TMAX	401	null	null	a	null
ASN00015643	20180101	TMIN	234	null	null	a	null
ASN00015643	20180101	PRCP	0	null	null	a	null

Figure 1: RECORDS dataset sample data

STATION	LATITUDE	LONGITUDE	ELEVATION	STATION_NAME
ASN00015643	-22.4518	133.6377	565.6	TERRITORY GRAPE FARM
CA1MB000296	49.8692	-97.4116	180.1	MB HEADINGLEY 0.6 SW - CANWARN
US1MISW005	-42.93	-84.1046	249.9	MI DURAND 6.2 WNW
ACW00011604	17.1167	-61.7833	10.1	ST JOHNS COOLIDGE FLD
ACW00011604	17.1333	-61.7833	19.2	ST JOHNS
AE000041196	25.333	55.517	34.0	SHARJAH INTER. AIRP

Figure 2: STATIONS dataset sample data

Looking to our small dataset and the documentation (**https://www1.ncdc.noaa.gov/pub/data/cdo/documentation/GHCND_documentation.pdf**) from NOAA, we can understand the questions and answers of researchers all around the world. Questions like these:

- What is the maximum temperature in Celsius (TMAX) at Sharjah International Airport (25.333° N, 55.517° E)?
- What is the rainiest place on earth (Observation = PRCP)?
- Assuming we load all the historical data from NOAA, what is the change in precipitation in a specific geographical location?
- How has the weather of a place changed in the last 100 years?

If you are a developer, your instinct may tell you our data looks like a well-known structure called a table, a concept from relational databases. If we present our dataset as a table, the design looks like this:

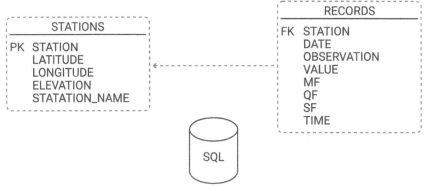

Figure 3: SQL view of the datasets

Within a relational database, you can use Structured Query Language or SQL to access data stored in the database. For example, if we want to know how many records we have in our data, we just have to execute:

```
> select count (*) from RECORDS
34126531
```

That one was easy, wasn't it? Counting the number of rows in a relational database is an easy operation; we just have to count to obtain our result. Another example is to obtain the different observation types used in the RECORDS dataset. We can execute:

```
> select distinct (OBSERVATION) from RECORDS LIMIT 10
WESD

TMIN

TMAX3

PRCP

SNOW
```

Distinct is another operation in relational databases; it returns the different values found in a column. What happens if in our data, we need to have more than one observation type? Our initial design works fine if we have just one observation, but in essence, the design of relational databases is too complex and difficult to change. Once it's designed, changing it might impact the whole design and applications using it. This is just one of the problems that drive the creation of NoSQL databases. If we suddenly need more than one observation type, what can we do? One might think we can store the observation types and values in an array. If you have worked with relational databases in the past, you know this is not a proper solution because our table is not normalized, and when we break normalization rules in relational databases, we are taking a path to disaster—but bear with me for a few minutes because there is a different point that I want to make.

STATION	DATE	OBSERVATION	VALUE	MF	QF	SF	TIME
US1MISW005	20180101	[PRCP, TMAX, TMIN]	[0, 513, 123]	null	null	N	null
CA1MB000296	20180101	[SNOW, TMAX, TMIN]	[0, 434, 67]	null	null	N	null
ASN00015643	20180101	[PRCP]	[0]	null	null	N	null

Figure 4: Observations and values using string arrays

What happens if we need to update a record? That's right, we have to use an operation called Update. Let's take a look at one example:

```
> update posts set OBSERVATIONS = '[ TMIN, TMAX]', VALUES = [634,
223] where STATION= 'US1MISW0005' AND DATE='20181013'
done
```

Specifically, we run an update that sets two tags in one cell within one row in our table. This is called fine-grained transformation. Imagine that you have a large dataset, a fine-grained transformation is a transformation that is applied to a smaller set, and it may be a single row. This is a scenario where relational databases are pretty good; you can insert, update and delete specific records, and you can execute queries to extract specific information. Even when relational databases work fine, there are a couple caveats when using databases. Let's study them in the next two sections.

Scalability

So far, we have used a small dataset with only four rows. Let's imagine you have millions of rows. When we are talking about large-scale data, let's say petabytes of information that grows every day, we have to take a few minutes to think about how and where we are going to store that information and how we are going to handle the data growth—and after that, even more important, how we are going to apply transformation in that data in an acceptable time frame.

One might think we can use a bigger box—by the way, that's called scale-up—but when we get more and more data, we will need bigger boxes more often. There are a lot of problems related to this approach, but maybe the most important one is the investment associated with getting bigger boxes. The price of large hardware is really high, so scale-up is not an option; if you follow this path, at some point you will find that there isn't a large enough box to handle your data.

After years of studying the problem, academic institutions and companies with big pockets and the ability to buy bigger hardware all decided the right path is to go for parallelism, called scale-out. What does that mean? Well, it means using many boxes, many of them commodity hardware, working together, communicating by high-speed networks to obtain a common result. We just have described in simple words one of the basic premises of Big Data: massively parallel computing. This is what Hadoop does as well as Spark. We will get into details in the next sections, but Spark is able to process large amounts of data by working in parallel.

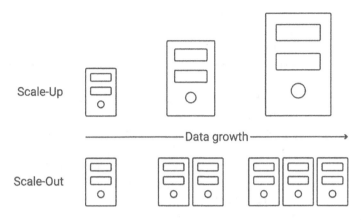

Figure 5: Scale-up vs Scale-out

Transformations

What is a transformation? Or, more precisely, coarse-grained transformations. To answer this question, let's take a look at one example. Imagine that you have the following dataset:

STATION	STATION_NAME
ASN00015643	TERRITORY GRAPE FARM
CA1MB000296	MB HEADINGLEY 0.6 SW - CANWARN
US1MISW005	MI DURAND 6.2 WNW
ACW00011604	ST JOHNS COOLIDGE FLD
ACW00011604	ST JOHNS
AE000041196	SHARJAH INTER. AIRP

Figure 6: Dataset

We want to perform a word count over the field STATION_NAME. With the size of this dataset (just six rows), it is easy to say that, for example, the number of times JOHNS appears in the dataset is two, and SHARJAH is one, and so on and so forth.

The algorithm to implement the word count is simple:

- Split each title by space.
- Remove punctuation marks.
- Group by word.
- Count how many times each word occurs.

That was easy, wasn't it? But what happens when we have millions or billions of rows?

Probably with the right dataset size, it would be possible to implement this algorithm in a general-purpose programming language like C++ and run it on a single computer. With that approach, we would be able to process a few million rows, but the limit is the amount of resources we have available. As we recall from the previous section, we have to look for a way to scale out.

Why do we need to worry about the data set size and whether it fits in the computer memory? We have Spark, and this simple problem can be addressed with a few transformations; the underlying cluster will take care of the rest. At this point, I'll give you an overview to introduce the process, concepts and some useful terminology.

To work with our data, we are going to use what is called an RDD, or a Resilient Distributed Dataset. It is the core original abstraction of Spark. For now, what is important to know about RDD is that it takes care of how data is distributed in the cluster and abstracts all the distributed system implementation and operations from the developer. It will automatically split the data into partitions and store each partition in different computers.

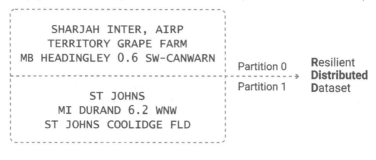

Figure 7: RDD

The algorithm using Spark is:

1. Read the data. There are multiple ways to do it, and there are multiple sources like memory, disk, cloud storage, network storage, etc. The data will be loaded into an RDD of strings, and the data will be distributed across the cluster.

2. Split each line by space *.split(" ")*. This step is performed using the transformation called *map*. This step will generate a new RDD of arrays of strings.

Figure 8: RDD of string arrays

3. Using the transformation *flatMap*, we will create an RDD of only strings

```
[SHARJAH, INTER, AIRP,
[TERRITORY, GRAPE, FARM,
[MB, HEADINGLEY, 0.6, SW-CANWARN]
```
Partition 0 → **Resilient Distributed** Dataset
Partition 1

```
[ST, JOHNS,
[MI, DURAND, 6.2, WNW,
[ST, JOHNS, COOLIDGE, FLD]
```

Figure 9: RDD of strings

Note: If you are familiar with Spark, you will notice that we can avoid Step 2 and use the *flatMap* of Step 3 with the *.split(" ")* function.

4. Now we need another map transformation to map each string to a number, in this case 1.

```
[(SHARJAH,1),(INTER,1),(AIRP,1),
(TERRITORY,1),(GRAPE,1),(FARM,1),
(MB,1),(HEADINGLEY,1),(0.6,1),(SW-CANWARN,1)]
```
Partition 0 → **Resilient Distributed** Dataset
Partition 1

```
[(ST,1),(JOHNS,1),
(MI,1),(DURAND,1),(6.2,1),(WNW,1),
(ST,1),(JOHNS,1),(COOLIDGE,1),(FLD,1)]
```

Figure 10: RDD of (string, 1)

5. Now we are going to perform another transformation called *reduceByKey*. It is going to count the words and sum the values. For example, if we have (RDD, 1) and (RDD, 1) in each partition, the reduceByKey will produce (RDD, 2).

6. Now what we need is an *action*, which triggers the application of all the transformations' computations and brings the distributed results from all the nodes, in this case *.collect()*, and the result is:

```
(SHARJAH,1)      (INTER,1)
(AIRP,1)         (TERRITORY,1)
(GRAPE,1)        (FARM,1)
(MB,1)           (HEADINGLEY,1)
(0.6,1)          (SW-CANWARN,1)
(ST,1)           (JOHNS,1)
(MI,1)           (DURAND,1)
(6.2,1)          (WNW,1)
(ST,1)           (JOHNS,1)
(COOLIDGE,1)     (FLD,1)
```

11

Figure 11: Result of the collect action

Now let's take a look at the Spark code:

```
>>> lines_rdd = sc.textFile('file:///tmp/records-sample.txt')

>>> words_rdd = lines_rdd.flatMap(lambda line: line.split(' '))

>>> word_num_rdd = words_rdd.map(lambda x: (x,1))

>>> word_num_rdd.reduceByKey(lambda x, y: x + y).collect()
[(u'COOLIDGE', 1), (u'FARM', 1), (u'MI', 1), (u'INTER.', 1),
(u'AIRP', 1), (u'DURAND', 1), (u'SHARJAH', 1), (u'GRAPE', 1),
(u'HEADINGLEY', 1), (u'MB', 1), (u'JOHNS', 2), (u'0.6', 1), (u'SW-
CANWARN', 1), (u'ST', 2), (u'WNW', 1), (u'TERRITORY', 1), (u'FLD',
1), (u'6.2', 1)]
```

This can be done with just one line of Spark code by chaining operations:

```
>>> lines_rdd = sc.textFile('file:///tmp/records-
sample.txt').flatMap(lambda line: line.split(' ')).map(lambda x:
(x,1)).reduceByKey(lambda x, y: x + y).collect()
[(u'COOLIDGE', 1), (u'FARM', 1), (u'MI', 1), (u'INTER.', 1),
(u'AIRP', 1), (u'DURAND', 1), (u'SHARJAH', 1), (u'GRAPE', 1),
(u'HEADINGLEY', 1), (u'MB', 1), (u'JOHNS', 2), (u'0.6', 1), (u'SW-
CANWARN', 1), (u'ST', 2), (u'WNW', 1), (u'TERRITORY', 1), (u'FLD',
1), (u'6.2', 1)]
```

Partitioning Data

Imagine if Spark performed the transformations in order on the entire dataset, how long it would take to process millions or even billions of records? I say it would be quite a bit. To reduce this time, the distributed computing Divide and Conquer algorithm design approach comes into play. Suppose we take our dataset and we divide it in half; each of the parts is called a partition, and it is just a logical partition of our data, but now we can process each partition in parallel.

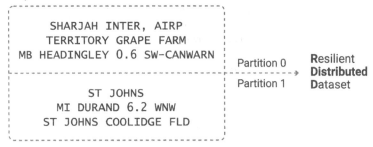

Figure 12: Dataset by half

We will go into detail in the following chapters, but for now, it is worth mentioning that the work will be done by an executor, which is just a process that runs in each of the nodes of the cluster and can perform a set of operations. The executor will receive the partition and apply all required transformations.

When we say the work will be executed in parallel and we split our dataset by half, it means that our process is going to take approximately half the time. There is one important question about Parallel Execution. How is it that Spark manages the scope and lifecycle of variables and methods when executing code in a cluster?

The answer is closures, which is the code and variables required to execute a computation in each distributed node over a partition of data. Whenever there is a task that will be executed in one of the worker nodes, the code that will be run is bundled up into a closure, and a copy is distributed to each worker node. If the code in one node modifies a local variable, this change is not reflected in other nodes. If you wanted to share among nodes, there are a couple of special variables called Broadcast variables and Accumulators that allow sharing of information between all nodes, which will be covered in later chapters.

There is another Spark concept called pipelines. With them we process out data in stages, and we don't wait for all the data to go through each transformation to start with the next one. Instead, Spark keeps passing data onto the next stages. Using pipelines increases the speed at which data is processed.

Data	Transformation 1	Transformation 2	Result
SHARJAH INTER, AIRP TERRITORY GRAPE FARM MB HEADINGLEY 0.6 SW-CANWARN	[SHARJAH,INTER,AIRP]		
			Partitions
ST JOHNS MI DURAND 6.2 WNW ST JOHNS COOLIDGE FLD	[ST,JOHNS]		

Figure 13: First iteration with pipelines

In Figure 13, we can observe that Spark started the computation in each partition. We apply the transformation *.map()* with the *.split(" ")* function to one of the records of each partition, and then Spark applies the same transformation to the next record in each partition, and at the same time, it applies the second transformation that is a *flatMap()* to the first processed records.

Data	Transformation 1	Transformation 2	Result
SHARJAH INTER, AIRP TERRITORY GRAPE FARM MB HEADINGLEY 0.6 SW-CANWARN	[SHARJAH,INTER,AIRP] [TERRITORY,GRAPE,FARM]	[(SHARJAH,1),(INTER,1),(AIRP,1)]	
			Partitions
ST JOHNS MI DURAND 6.2 WNW ST JOHNS COOLIDGE FLD	[ST,JOHNS] [MI,DURAND,6.2,WNW]	[(ST,1),(JOHNS,1)]	

Figure 14: Second iteration using pipelines

Let's compare how the processing is done under different circumstances. First, without distributed systems; let's call it *one at a time;* second is *parallel,* where distributed systems come into play; and third is *parallel with pipeline*, the method used by Spark. Let's take a look at Figure 14.

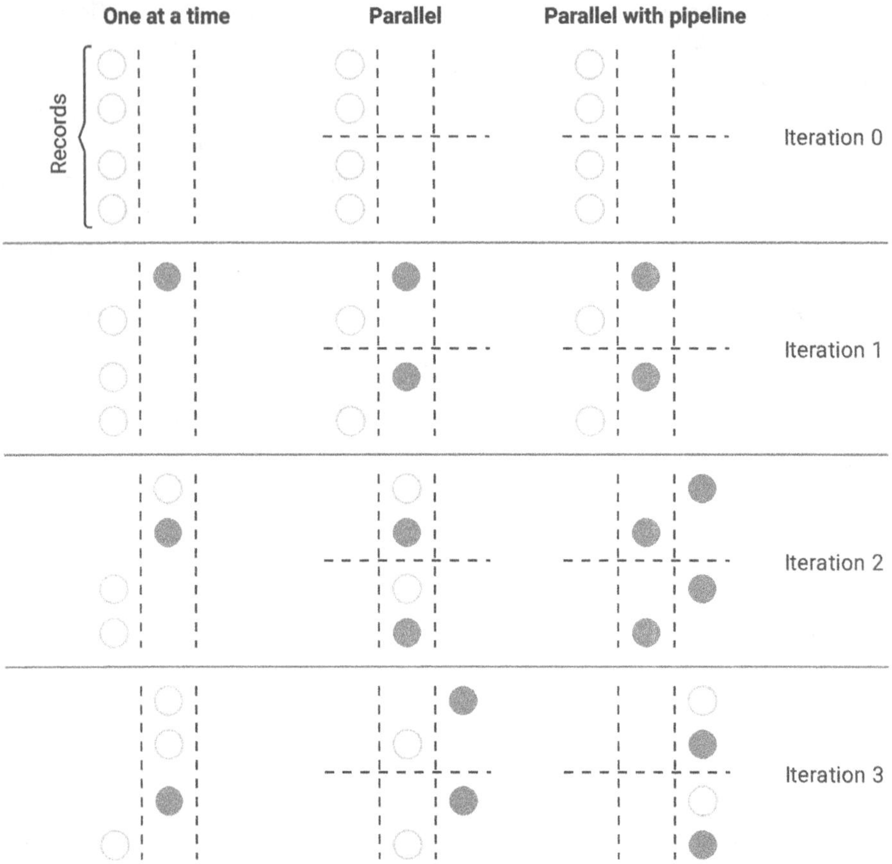

Figure 15: Processing approaches

With a dataset of just four records and two transformations, after three iterations, *parallel with pipeline* has finished the work, while *one at a time* has processed three records of the first transformation, and *parallel* has finished with the first transformation for all the records but just two records of the second transformation. Just imagine the processing performance when you have hundreds of transformations and billions of records in the dataset.

Narrow and Wide Transformations

Sometimes, the data in one state is transformed to the next state, while the more important data remains independent. If we recall the example that we have been using, we have four records in our dataset and two partitions with two records each. When we process the first record of the first partition, it doesn't have any iteration, dependency or relation with the other records in the dataset. This is what is called *narrow transformation*. In our example, when we apply *.map()* and *.flatMap()*, those are narrow transformations.

When we apply a transformation where there are dependencies between records within the same partition or in different partitions in order to obtain the result, we call it a *wide transformation*, for example reduceByKey. Imagine that we have the following dataset:

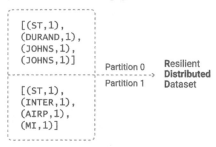

Figure 16: reduceByKey dataset

If we apply a reduceByKey, for example, we have to check whether there are several instances of the same key across partitions. For example, we have two records that have *ST* as key, and those records are in different partitions. In this case, data must be moved around multiple partitions when doing a transformation, and this is a *wide transformation*.

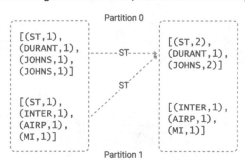

15

Figure 17: reduceByKey example

For now, the important part is that this process of moving data between partitions is called *shuffle*, but not always when you have to shuffle data it is a wide transformation.

It is important to avoid using wide transformations; this is because if we have only narrow transformations in our pipeline, our data processing will be fast, but if we add wide transformations to our equation, the processing time will increase.

Lineage

A Spark program is a collection of transformations applied to an RDD. Each transformation produces a new RDD, and internally this is represented as a *lineage graph*. An RDD lineage is defined as a "graph of *transformation* operations required to execute when an *action* is called." It is also known as an RDD operator graph or RDD dependency graph. From this graph, we get a logical execution plan.

A logical execution plan is represented as a direct acyclic graph (DAG), where multiple vertices or nodes represent an RDD and many edges represent the transformations applied to the RDDs. It is important to mention that a DAG doesn't contain cycles, and it is finite, which means it has a beginning and an end. The graph starts with *data input* to load data into an RDD and is finished with an *action* that triggers the computation.

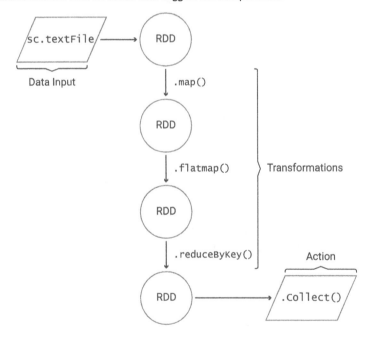

Figure 18: Lineage graph

Spark Laziness

Spark is lazy, and the term "lazy evaluation" means the computation is triggered when an action is called. Any of the transformations or even data input are called until that point. Something important regarding laziness is that Spark can perform optimizations in the graph or the code that is going to be executed; Spark knows all the transformations and actions to be executed in advance so it can decide the best way to execute the logical execution plan.

Resiliency

RDDs are not just like an array or structure to hold data; they are way more than that. RDDs contain a set of instructions that are used to materialize and transform the data and generate results with the operations being performed in parallel.

What happens if one of the cluster nodes fails? It is just going to request resources in another node to apply the transformation over the partition, and this doesn't apply only to failed nodes. If Spark detects one node is slow, it can request to move the computation to another node.

Xavier Morera & Nereo Campos

3 Getting Technical with Spark

In the previous chapter, we started to understand Spark with a high-level overview, and we studied the characteristics that make Spark the best cluster computing framework. In this chapter, we will start getting technical. We are going to study Spark's architecture, components, APIs and core abstractions, and we will learn how to develop a Spark application.

Spark's Architecture

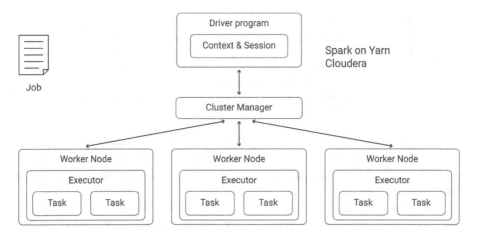

Figure 19: Spark's architecture

In Figure 19, we can observe the multiple components that must be understood when working with Spark. There are some differences, depending on whether you are working with Spark standalone or Spark cluster (using YARN or Apache Mesos). We are going to focus on the components of our working environment, a Cloudera Cluster using YARN.

- **Spark Driver/Driver Program:** The main piece of software in charge of managing everything that takes place when executing a Spark Application, it is the master node of our application. One of its main tasks is to create the lineage graph, or execution graph, and split it into multiple stages, depending on the transformations and actions that will be applied to our data. It also exposes the Spark UI, a lightweight web application that provides information that is important to know about our Spark Environment and information about the job and stages we are executing. Its key responsibility is to negotiate the resource allocation with the cluster manager and then create small execution units called *Tasks*, which are divided into the available resources in the cluster.

- **Spark Context/Spark Session:** Residing inside the Spark Driver, it is the entry point for any application to the Spark Environment when using RDDs (Spark Context) or SparkSQL (Spark Session). When using REPL, the context and session are created for you.
- **Cluster Manager:** In charge of getting resources for execution and allocating them for a particular job. In the case of Cloudera, YARN is used as a cluster manager. YARN stands for *Yet Another Resource Negotiator*.
- **Job:** An application that has been submitted to the cluster and uses Spark Context or Spark Session to interact with the Spark Environment.
- **Worker Nodes:** As their name states, they are nodes that do work. Spark has a master-slave architecture; the Spark Driver becomes the master, and the worker nodes the slaves. Each worker node can have one or many executors that will be dependent on the available resources.
- **Executor:** Receives a *closure* that contains the piece of software that represents the *task* to be executed. The executors are in charge of reading and writing from and to data sources. They perform data processing and store intermediate computation results in disk or memory. Executors are created and registered within the driver program, and additional executors can be requested when needed.
- **Task:** Bite-size units of work that the Spark Driver sends for execution. There is one task per executor.

Whenever you submit an application, all those components are required to run your job. But we are missing an important part of any architecture: *storage* is the final piece that we need to be able to run our jobs. Something important is that Spark is a large-scale engine for data processing, but one important design decision was not to create a storage layer. Instead, it uses existing ones. For that reason, Spark can connect to several storage services like HDFS, Local Filesystems, Amazon S3, Azure Blob Storage, Google Cloud Storage, Elasticsearch, Cassandra and MongoDB, just to mention some of them. Spark can connect natively to some storage services, while in other cases a connector is required. It is valuable to mention that HDFS is the most used storage service, in large part because many of the Data Lakes were being processed with Hadoop, but cloud storage services like Amazon S3 are gaining ground because they have proven themselves to be incredibly reliable and fast and more cost efficient than HDFS.

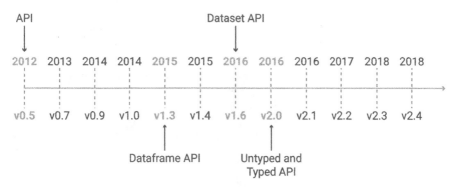

Figure 20: Spark API and version release history

Spark's APIs

Ever since the first version of Spark, version v0.5, RDDs have been the core abstraction of Spark. RDDs have proven to be extremely powerful and useful, allowing you to apply coarse-grained transformations over your datasets in a massively parallel and resilient fashion. When using RDDs, you have to specify exactly what you want to do with your data. For this reason, when you use RDDs, your data is a black box for Spark, so there are a lot of limitations in the optimizations that could be made. In terms of structured data, it is not possible to infer schema based on data. If you are working with RDDs, don't worry; Spark really believes in backward compatibility.

In 2015, a new version of Spark came to life, version v1.3, and a new abstraction called *DataFrame* was introduced, originally called *SchemaRDD*. A DataFrame is similar to an RDD in that it is an immutable distributed set of data, but with the difference that it organizes the data in named columns. Just like a database, it allows the user to query the data with a well-known and worldwide-accepted language, SQL. In 2016, version v1.6 was released and introduced a new abstraction called *Dataset*, which is basically a strongly typed DataFrame.

For version v2.0, released in 2016, the *DataFrame* and *Dataset* APIs were merged into one, making it easy to work with Spark. The DataFrame API basically became an untyped Dataset, namely Dataset of Row.

21

So, the important question here is "When should I use a DataFrame or an RDD?" Let's check the following table to help you make your decision:

RDD	DataFrame
Unstructured data	Structured or semi-structured data
Data manipulation with lambdas	Much easier to understand
Low-level transformations	Equivalent to a database table
Functional Programing Style	Leverage optimizations
	Relational Programming Style

Figure 21: RDDs vs DataFrame

Optimizations

There are two main components that can perform optimizations in Spark:

- **Catalyst Optimizer:** A framework that is part of SparkSQL, it optimizes queries, improving the performance. It was built with two principles in mind: 1) to allow adding new optimization techniques easily and 2) to enable external developers to extend the optimizer. The way the optimizer works is:

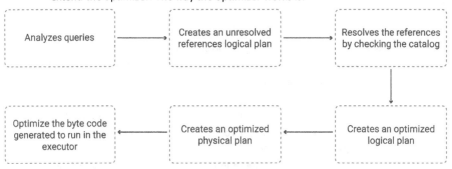

Figure 22: Catalyst optimizer

- **Project Tungsten:** Focuses on the hardware where Spark jobs are executed. It optimizes the code for CPU and memory efficiency, because these are the hardware components that are not growing at the same rate as others like Storage and Memory. The main features of Tungsten row format are:
  - o Optimizes data representation in memory.
  - o Allows managing memory explicitly.
  - o Exploits cache locality.
  - o Compiles to bytecode several expressions together instead of having to evaluate each expression one by one.

Spark Context

Spark Context is located in the Spark Driver, and it is the entry point for working with RDDs. You can use only one Spark Context per application, and in essence, it is the Spark application. When you are interacting with Spark using Spark Shell or REPL, Spark Context is created for you, but when you use Spark Submit, you have to create the Spark Context. Let's check how to create the Spark Context in code.

```
from pyspark import SparkConf, SparkContext
conf = (SparkConf().setMaster("yarn").setAppName("Test App")
  .set("spark.executor.memory", "2g"))
sc = SparkContext(conf=conf)
```

Spark Session

It is the main entry point when working with SparkSQL. In other words, when working with DataFrames or Datasets, it merges the *SQL Context* and *Hive Context* into one object and allows you to access the Spark Context. You can have multiple Spark Sessions per application, but only one Spark Context per JVM. The Spark Session is created for you when you are working in Spark Shell or REPL, and you have to create it when you use Spark Submit. Let's check how to create the SparkSession in code.

```
from pyspark import SparkConf, SparkSession
spark = SparkSession.builder.master("yarn").appName("Test App")
  .config("spark.submit.deployMode", "").
.config("spark.executor.memory", "2g").getOrCreate()
```

Spark Configuration

There are three locations to configure in Spark: *properties*, which control application parameters, *environment variables*, which set per machine settings, and *logging* via log4j.properties. We will be setting application parameters when fine-tuning our Spark application, and there are several ways of doing it:

- **spark-defaults.conf:** Each time an application is executed, it is the first source of configuration.
- **Command line:** When you execute your application using spark-submit or in standalone mode, you can pass flags,s and those values overwrite the ones in spark-defaults.conf.
- **Code:** Properties can be set by code, and these properties have the highest precedence. For example, in the previous section's code snippets, we used *SparkConf* to pass application parameters to Spark Context and Spark Session.

Spark on YARN: The Cluster Manager

YARN is a cluster manager technology; it stands for Yet Another Resource Negotiator, and it was developed as Hadoop Next Generation or Hadoop 2.0. Its two main tasks are:
- Managing resources (CPU/Memory) in the cluster.
- Scheduling and monitoring jobs.

How do the cluster manager and Spark applications interact? Well, the following things happen when you submit a Spark Application from your workstation:
- The driver program will start in one of the cluster's nodes.
- The driver program contacts the Resource Manager to submit the job.
- The resource manager inspects the job and its constraints and negotiates with the Node Manager from the worker nodes to determine where it can start a container that will have the application master.
- Once the application master is up and running, the resource manager will communicate with it to inform it where in the cluster there are resources available to do the work.
- The application master will communicate with the node manager where resources are available; here the containers are created.
- The containers register with the application master as executors and perform the work (tasks) received from the Spark Driver.

Something important to mention is that there are even resource scheduling modes like FIFO (first-in, first-out) or Fair Scheduler, and they can be modified to your needs.

Dataset

In this book, we will run several examples to show the different capabilities of Spark. For all the examples, we will use datasets from the National Centers for Environmental Information (NOOA, **https://www.ncdc.noaa.gov/**), specifically the datasets from Global Historical Climatology Network (GHCN). We will use the following datasets:
- **GHCND Stations:**

Location: **https://www1.ncdc.noaa.gov/pub/data/ghcn/daily/ghcnd-stations.txt**

Contains information about the stations around the world that collect daily information related to weather, and it contains 108,081 records. From now on, we will refer to this dataset as STATIONS. It contains the following columns:
  - **STATION:** Type String. It is the unique identifier of a station.
  - **LATITUDE:** Type Double
  - **LONGITUDE:** Type Double
  - **ELEVATION:** Type Double
  - **STATION_NAME:** Type String

- **GHCN 2018:**

Location: **https://www1.ncdc.noaa.gov/pub/data/ghcn/daily/by_year/2018.csv.gz**

Contains information collected every day, and it is grouped by year. The file size is about 1.1GB, and it contains about 34,126,531 records. From now on, we will refer to this dataset as RECORDS. It contains the following columns:

- o **STATION:** Type String. It is the unique identifier of a station.
- o **DATE:** Type String. It represents a date with the format YYYYMMDD.
- o **OBSERVATION:** Type String. It represents the name of the type of weather observation; a complete list of observation types can be found in the following URL: **https://www1.ncdc.noaa.gov/pub/data/cdo/documentation/GHCND_documentation.pdf**
- o **VALUE:** Type Integer. It contains the value of the observation.
- o **MF:** Type String. It contains the Measurement Flag, which defines the attributes of the observation collected.
- o **QF:** Type String. It contains the Quality Flag, which indicates whether the collected data passed quality tests.
- o **SF:** Type String. It contains the Source Flag, which defines the type of source where the observation was performed.
- o TIME: Type String. It contains the time of the observation in format HHMM.

Xavier Morera & Nereo Campos

4 Spark's RDDs

Resilient Distributed Dataset or RDD is the original core abstraction of Spark. It is worth mentioning that developing applications using RDDs is not the recommended way to go; instead, you might have an easier time getting started with DataFrames and SparkSQL. In terms of performance, there are several optimizations that are applied to DataFrames that cannot be applied to RDDs. Having said that, I believe it is better to start with the core low-level API before you start digging into high-level APIs, for the following reasons:

- RDDs are still used internally. Understanding RDDs helps you to have a better foundation of the inner workings of Spark.
- There may be cases where something that you want to do is not possible with DataFrames and you need to fall back to RDDs.
- There is a lot of code written using RDDs, and it may be part of your job to maintain and extend that code.

Recall from the previous chapter that SparkContext is the entry point of the RDD API, namely Spark Core. You need the SparkContext to run your application. It is created for you using REPL when running Spark or PySpark shell, but you need to create it when you want to submit your application to a Spark Cluster using spark submit. Spark Context allows you to configure all necessary parameters regarding your application configuration and environment, it sets up the internal services required for your application to run, and it provides methods to help you to create RDDs and start applying transformations to your data.

Let's check some of the features of the Spark Context:

- Execute *PySpark*. When you execute it, it will show two messages:
  - "To adjust logging level use *sc.setLogLevel(newLevel)*." Notice that it is using Spark Context as sc.
  - "SparkSession available as 'spark.'"
- *dir(sc)* can be used to inspect the attributes of the Spark Context.
- Each attribute can be inspected by separately executing *sc.<attribute name>*, for example *sc.serializer* or *sc.sparkUser*.
- Spark Context can be stopped by executing *sc.stop()*.
- Spark Context can be recreated using *sc = SparkContext.getOrCreate()*.
- An empty RDD can be created using *empty_rdd = sc.emptyRDD()*.

```
$pyspark
Python 2.7.15
Using Spark's default log4j profile: org/apache/spark/log4j-
defaults.properties Setting default log level to "WARN". To adjust
logging level use sc.setLogLevel(newLevel).
SparkSession available as 'spark'.

>>> dir(sc)
['PACKAGE_EXTENSIONS', '__class__', '__delattr__', … , 'union',
'version', 'wholeTextFiles']

>>> sc.serializer
AutoBatchedSerializer(PickleSerializer())

>>> sc.sparkUser
<bound method SparkContext.sparkUser of <SparkContext
master=local[*] appName=PySparkShell>>

>>> empty_rdd = sc.emptyRDD()

>>> sc.stop()

>>> sc = SparkContext.getOrCreate()
```

This is just an overview of what you can do with Spark. In the next sections we will go deeper into transformations and actions that we can apply to RDDs.

Resilient Distributed Datasets

Figure 23: Types of RDDs

There are many types of RDDs, as we can see in Figure 22, and you can create your own RDDs. All of them share five important properties we have to bear in mind when we work with Spark:

- **Partitions:** When using RDDs, your data is divided into subsets of data. Each subset is called a partition. This way multiple executors can work on your data independently. Each partition is processed by an executor. There is a concept called Speculative Tasks; sometimes several executors can repeat the same computation, and Spark will choose the one that finishes first. If an executor fails, another one can perform the job.
- **Dependencies:** Spark keeps track of the parent RDDs of an RDD. This way we can define dependencies between RDDs. This can be observed with the lineage graph, where you can see the RDDs and the transformations that generated new RDDs.
- **Functions to compute partition:** Used to recreate a partition in case of failure, the function is applied to the entire dataset and generates a set of partitions.
- **Partitioner:** Defines the way the data is divided in any partitioner of the form (key, value) pair.
- **Preferred locations for compute:** Remember, one of the basic premises of Big Data is taking computation to the data; well, with this property, an RDD can specify where the partition should live.

Each RDD type is defined by its properties and the data it handles, for instance *PairRDDs*, the main purpose of which is to contain (key, value) pairs. Each entry is a tuple; it is useful for grouping and aggregating, and it has available specialized transformations. Before you create your own RDD, verify all the existing ones, and make sure there isn't one that fills your needs.

Creating RDDs

There are three primary ways of creating RDDs:

- Using *parallelize()* will create an RDD in memory from data you provide or specify.
- From an external data source, for example reading objects from S3 or HDFS.
- From another RDD. Given that RDDs are immutable objects, whenever you apply a transformation, a new RDD will be created.

Parallelize

For this method, we will take a collection or iterable, for example a list, and we will use the method *parallelize()* to create an RDD in this particular case of type ParallelCollectionRDD. Then we use the action *collect()* to bring the data from all the worker nodes to your machine and display them. Be careful with *collect()* because if your dataset is too big, it will cause memory issues.

```
>>> list_one_to_five = sc.parallelize([1,2,3,4,5])

>>> list_one_to_five
ParallelCollectionRDD[3] at parallelize at PythonRDD.scala:489

>>> list_one_to_five.collect()
[1, 2, 3, 4, 5]

>>> list_one_to_five.getNumPartitions()
4

>>> list_one_to_five_one_partition = sc.parallelize([1,2,3,4,5], 1)

>>> list_one_to_five_one_partition.getNumPartitions()
1

>>> dir(list_one_to_five)
...

>>> list_one_to_five.sum()
15

>>> list_one_to_five.max()
5

>>> list_one_to_five.min()
1

>>> list_one_to_five.mean()
3.0

>>> bigger_rdd = sc.parallelize(range(1,1000))

>>> bigger_rdd.sum()
499500
```

Sometimes it is important to know how many partitions we have, and we can use the method *getNumPartitions()* to obtain that. Also, when we use *parallelize()*, we can specify the number of partitions we want to use. Using the method *dir()*, we can inspect the attributes of the RDD. Using the *range()* function, we can create even bigger collections. Finally, we can apply operations in the RDD, like *sum(), max(), min() and mean()*, and there are more actions and transformations we can apply to RDDs.

Something important to mention is that RDDs can hold different types of objects, even tuples or collections. This is probably the biggest difference with DataFrames.

External Data Source

Data can be loaded from an external data source, for example from HDFS or Local File System. In this case, we are going to use *.textFile()* to load data from an external data source, in this case our local file system.

```
>>> sc.textFile("file:///tmp/numbers.txt")

>>> list_one_to_five

>>> list_one_to_five
ParallelCollectionRDD[3] at parallelize at PythonRDD.scala:489

>>> list_one_to_five_one_partition =
list_one_to_five.repartition(1)

>>> list_one_to_five.getNumPartitions()
4

>>> list_one_to_five_one_partition.getNumPartitions()
1

>>> list_one_to_five.isEmpty()
False

>>> empty_rdd=sc.emptyRDD()

>>> empty_rdd.isEmpty()
True
```

Using the method *repartition()*, we can create a new RDD from another RDD and specify the number of partitions we want to use. Using *isEmpty()*, we may check whether an RDD is empty, and using the method *sc.emptyRDD()*, we can create an empty RDD.

From another RDD

We can use transformations to create new RDDs, for example:

```
>>>list_one_to_five = sc.parallelize([1,2,3,4,5])

>>>list_tuples = list_one_to_five.map(lambda x:(x,1))

>>>list_tuples.collect()
[(1,1),(2,1),(3,1),(4,1),(5,1)]
```

In this case we use the *.map()* function to create a new RDD. We can create as many RDDs as we want.

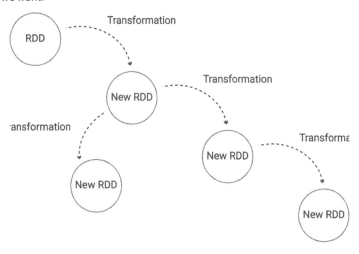

Figure 24: Apply transformations to RDDs

Each time we apply a transformation, a new RDD comes to life; remember, RDDs are immutable.

Returning Data to the Driver

Most of the time what happens is that you have your data, and you run the Spark application, and then the result is saved for future use on disk, in HDFS or in a NoSQL store. When we are interacting with Spark using PySpark or Spark Shell, it's important to display something to the console. We want to get results, review them and keep working. Remember, we are working in a distributed environment; we have to retrieve data from all the partitions. For this there are several commands that can be used, for example:

```
>>> sc.textFile("file:///tmp/numbers.txt")

>>> bigger_rdd = sc.parallelize(range(1,1000))

>>> bigger_rdd.collect()
[1, 2, 3, 4, 5, 6, 7, 8, 9, 10 … 999]

>>> bigger_rdd.take(3)
[1, 2, 3]

>>> bigger_rdd.first()
1

>>> bigger_rdd.takeOrdered(10, key=lambda x: -x)
[999, 998, 997, 996, 995, 994, 993, 992, 991, 990]

>>> tuple_rdd = bigger_rdd.map(lambda x: (x,1))

>>> tuple_map = tuple_rdd.collectAsMap()

>>> type(tuple_map)
<type 'dict'>

>>> for element in bigger_rdd.take(10):
    print element
1
…
10
```

- **collect():** Brings all data from all partitions to the driver program, potentially can cause a memory exception on large datasets.
- **take():** Receives as a parameter the number of rows of data to retrieve.
- **first():** Returns the first element or one of the partitions.
- **takeOrdered():** Receives the number of rows of data to return and the function to order the data.
- **collectAsMap():** Returns the (key, value) pairs in this RDD to the master as a Python map.

Partition Operations

There are three important operations when working with partitions:
- **getNumPartitions():** Displays the number of partitions of the RDD.
- **Repartition():** Creates a new RDD with a different number of partitions.
- **coalesce():** Creates a new RDD with fewer partitions; it cannot increase the number of partitions. In the example, when we try to execute "list_one_to_five.coalesce(5).getNumPartitions()" it continues saying 4 because the number of the partition in *list_one_to_five* is 4 and *coalesce* cannot increment it. Something really important is that coalesce tries to avoid shuffle.

```
>>> list_one_to_five = sc.parallelize([1,2,3,4,5])

>>> one_partition = list_one_to_five.repartition(1)

>>> two_partition = list_one_to_five.repartition(2)

>>> list_one_to_five.getNumPartitions()
4

>>> one_partition.getNumPartitions()
1

>>> two_partition.getNumPartitions()
2

>>> list_one_to_five.coalesce(5).getNumPartitions()
4

>>> list_one_to_five.coalesce(3).getNumPartitions()
3

>>> list_one_to_five.repartition(3)
    .saveAsTextFile("file:///tmp/list_one_to_five")
```

One important method, *saveAsTextFile()*, allows Spark to save data in each partition as a text file. In the example, the data is going to be stored in the folder called */tmp/list_one_to_five*. If you execute an *ls* or *dir* command in that folder, you will get something like: "*_SUCCESS   part-00000   part-00001   part-00002.*"

Creating RDDs from External Data Sources

There are many data stores and formats that Spark can read and write, either natively or with the use of connectors. Spark can read from a local file system, HDFS, S3, Azure, Cassandra or Elasticsearch, to name some of them, and some of the supported formats are

CSV, XML, AVRO, Parquet, and JSON. Data that is loaded into Spark gets distributed into multiple partitions; it can be processed in parallel, and transformations and actions can be applied to create new RDDs and obtain results. Let's see some examples with the most common file formats.

Text File

To load data from text files, we can use the method *textFile()*. If you specify a folder, it loads all the files in the folder, but you can specify a single file.

```
>>> sc.textFile("/tmp/test/data").count()
1000

>>> sc.textFile("/tmp/test/ten").count()
10

>>> sc.textFile("/tmp/test/four").count()
4

>>> sc.textFile("/tmp/four/part-00000").count()
1
```

When running Spark on YARN, paths default to HDFS. That's why you don't have to specify "hdfs:/// …" but if you are using a different cluster manager, it will be required.

HDFS

HDFS stands for Hadoop Distributed File System. It is the primary storage system for Hadoop. If you ever wrote map/reduce applications, you used HDFS. HDFS is fault tolerant; it has a data replication schema, where if one node fails, other copies of data are available to be used. Data is divided into blocks, and the blocks are used by Spark for data partitioning. Spark has data locality, and it is exploded by having executors where the partitions reside. This way, data is not moved between nodes in the network. HDFS is optimized for parallel data processing.

Local Data

In order to work with local data, you have to specify *file://* before the file or path you want to load. Something important is that if you are in cluster mode, the file must be present in all the nodes of the cluster in the same location.

```
>>> local_play = sc.textFile("file:///stackexchange/play_part/")

>>> local_play.count()

>>> local_play.take(10)
```

CSV Files

When working with formats like CSV (Comma-Separated Values), it is important to specify the location of the JAR with the functionally needed to work with those formats. For example, if the JAR to work with CSV is located in /tmp/, you have to add to *spark-submit* command following the parameters *--packages /tmp/spark-csv.jar*. CSV files are plain text that can be opened and inspected with any text editor. It presents tabular data and can be opened with Excel; for example, despite the name, it supports different separators. For example, we can specify TAB instead of a comma.

Another approach is to load the file where each line of the file is a row of data and you can define a function to split each line by the separator. Let's execute the following example using our STATIONS dataset:

```
>>> stations_rdd = sc.textFile("/tmp/ghcnd-stations.csv")

>>> stations_rdd.take(2)
[u'STATION, LATITUDE, LONGITUDE, ELEVATION, STATION_NAME',
u'ACW00011604, 17.1167, -61.7833, 10.1, ST JOHNS COOLIDGE FLD ']

>>> def split_the_line(x):
    return x.split(',')

>>> stations_rdd_csv = stations_rdd.map(split_the_line)

>>> stations_rdd_csv.take(2)
[
[u'STATION', u' LATITUDE', u' LONGITUDE', u' ELEVATION', u'
STATION_NAME'],
    [u'ACW00011604', u' 17.1167', u' -61.7833', u' 10.1', u' ST
JOHNS COOLIDGE FLD']
]
```

JSON Files

Similar to CSV, every row is a JSON document, and you have to load the file and then parse each row. For example:

```
>>> stations_rdd = sc.textFile("/tmp/ghcnd-stations.json")

>>> stations_rdd.first()
u'{
"STATION":"ACW00011604",
"LATITUDE":17.1167,
"LONGITUDE":-61.7833,
"ELEVATION":10.1,
"STATION_NAME":" ST JOHNS COOLIDGE FLD"
}'
```

There are a bunch of libraries you can use to parse JSON, and you can use any of those inside a map to extract the information from the JSON documents.

S3 – Simple Storage Service

This is Amazon's cloud storage service; it is easy to create buckets and upload objects. Why should we use it? Because it has a rock-solid SLA, and its durability, availability and scalability are amazing. One good thing is that you pay only for what you use. In your AWS account, you have to enable programmatic access by using Access Keys and Secret Keys, or if you have your cluster in AWS, you can configure instance roles with access to the S3 buckets. The steps to use S3 are:

- Create an S3 bucket.
- Upload your datasets to your bucket.
- Create an IAM user to enable programmatic access.
- Obtain Access Key ID and Secret Access Key.
- Configure the keys in your environment; they must be configured in each node of your cluster.
- Load the necessary packages to access AWS, in this case hadoop-aws.jar file. You can look for it in the Maven Repository.

```
# Configure AWS access on your environment, the simplest way:
# export AWS_ACCESS_KEY_ID="access-key"
# export AWS_SECRET_ACCESS_KEY="secret-key"

>>> stations_rdd = sc.textFile("s3a://{S3BUCKET NAME}/data/ghcnd-
stations.json")

>>> stations_rdd.first()
u'{
"STATION":"ACW00011604",
"LATITUDE":17.1167,
"LONGITUDE":-61.7833,
"ELEVATION":10.1,
"STATION_NAME":" ST JOHNS COOLIDGE FLD"
}'
```

Saving Data

Let's take a look at the ways to save RDDs in Spark:

```
>>> def split_the_line(x):
    return x.split(',')

>>> stations_rdd = sc.textFile("/tmp/ghcnd-stations.csv")

>>> stations_rdd_csv = stations_rdd.map(split_the_line)

>>> stations_rdd_csv.saveAsTextFile("/tmp/stations_txt")

>>> stations_rdd_csv.saveAsPickleFile("/tmp/stations_pickle")

>>> stations_from_txt = sc.textFile("/tmp/stations_txt ")

>>> stations_from_pickle = sc.pickleFile("/tmp/stations_pickle ")

>>> stations_rdd_csv.count()
108082

>>> stations_from_txt.count()
108082

>>> stations_from_pickle.count()
108082
```

First, we load data from the local filesystem, and we split each line by comma. Using the method *saveAsTextFile()*, we save the file as text. When we use this method, any of the file metadata is stored in the file, and each row is saved only as text. The second method we use is *saveAsPickleFile()*. It uses Python pickle, a module for serializing (pickling) and deserializing (unpickling) objects. By pickling we preserve the object and all its metadata; you do not lose your transformations. Actually, when you *saveAsPickleFile()*, it is saved as a *SequenceFile* of pickled objects.

Sequence Files

SequenceFiles are flat files in binary format. They consist of key-value pairs, and they are used extensively in Hadoop. Here is an example of how we can directly use it:

```
>>> def split_the_line(x):
    return x.split(',')

>>> stations_rdd = sc.textFile("/tmp/ghcnd-stations.csv")

>>> stations_rdd_csv = stations_rdd.map(split_the_line)

>>> stations_rdd_csv.take(2)
[[u'ACW00011604', u' 17.1167', u' -61.7833', u' 10.1', u' ST JOHNS
COOLIDGE FLD '], [u'ACW00011647', u' 17.1333', u' -61.7833', u'
19.2', u' ST JOHNS ']]

>>> stations_rdd_sorted=stations_rdd_csv.sortBy(lambda line:
line[4])

>>> stations_rdd_sorted.saveAsSequenceFile("/tmp/ghcnd-
stations.seq")

>>> stations_rdd_seq = sc.sequenceFile("/tmp/ghcnd-stations.seq")

>>> stations_rdd_seq.take(2)
[(u'ASN00040708', u' -26.0336', u' 151.0603', u' 385.0', u' "HOME"
MONOGORILBY '), (u'ASN00039031', u' -24.6486', u' 150.7450', u'
404.8', u' "KAGEON" DAWES ')]
```

You can use *saveAsSequenceFile()* to save your RDD as a SequenceFile, and *sequenceFile()* to read Sequence Files.

Hadoop has several formats; you can define the input format that specifies how the input files are read and parsed. We also have output formats that specify how the files are written to storage. Using the method *saveAsNewApiHadoopFile(),* you can specify the formats. For example:

```
>>> stations_rdd_csv.saveAsNewAPIHadoopFile(("/tmp/ghcnd-
stations.hadoop"),
"org.apache.hadoop.mapreduce.lib.output.SequenceFileOutputFormat",
"org.apache.hadoop.io.IntWritable", "org.apache.hadoop.io.Text")

>>> stations_xml = sc.newAPIHadoopFile("/tmp/ghcnd-stations.xml,
'com.databricks.spark.xml.XmlInputFormat',
'org.apache.hadoop.io.Text', 'org.apache.hadoop.io.Text',
conf={'xmlinput.start':'<row','xmlinput.end':'/>'})
```

To load and save data, we have the following methods:

Load	Save
textFile()	saveAsTextFile()
pickleFile()	saveAsPickleFile()
sequenceFile()	saveAsSequenceFile()
hadoopFile()	saveAsHadoopFile()
hadoopDataset()	saveAsHadoopDataset()
newAPIHadoopFile()	saveAsNewAPIHadoopFile()

5 Going Deeper into Spark Core

So far, we have covered a lot of ground with Spark Core. If you are just getting started with Big Data, we can safely say that you are no longer a stranger to Spark. In the previous chapter, we focused primarily on the many ways of loading and saving data with RDDs. Now, it is time to go deeper into Spark Core. We will focus on transformations, actions, and partitions and look into learning more about sampling, combining, aggregating, set operations, caching, shared variables, and more.

Functions in Spark

There are two types of functions we can use in Spark transformations; the first one is named "functions." In the previous chapter, we applied the following function:

```
>>> stations_rdd = sc.textFile("/tmp/ghcnd-stations.csv")

>>> def split_the_line(x):
    return x.split(',')

>>> stations_rdd_csv = stations_rdd.map(split_the_line)

>>> stations_rdd_csv.take(2)
[[[u'ACW00011604', u' 17.1167', u' -61.7833', u' 10.1', u' ST JOHNS
COOLIDGE FLD '], [u'ACW00011647', u' 17.1333', u' -61.7833', u'
19.2', u' ST JOHNS ']]
```

In this example, we applied the function *split_the_line()* in the map transformation, so basically we defined the function and passed it as a parameter to the map transformation. The map transformation applies the function to each element of each partition. This works quite well, but we have a second function borrowed from functional programming, called anonymous functions or lambdas. Basically, you can specify a function inline when you define a transformation; it is a very lightweight method of creating functions. It's easy to read and easy to understand. For example, we can define the previous code as follows:

```
>>> stations_rdd = sc.textFile("/tmp/ghcnd-stations.csv")

>>> stations_rdd.take(2)
[u'ACW00011604, 17.1167, -61.7833, 10.1, ST JOHNS COOLIDGE FLD ']

>>> stations_rdd.map(lambda x: x.split(',')).take(2)
[[u'ACW00011604', u' 17.1167', u' -61.7833', u' 10.1', u' ST JOHNS
COOLIDGE FLD ']]
```

As you can see, we defined the function *split_the_line()* inside the map definition using the keyword *lambda*.

Bear lambda functions in mind; you will find yourself using lambdas all the time when working with Spark.

Transformations:

Next, we will review some of the more commonly used transformations.

map(f)

You pass a named function, or lambda function f, and it returns a new RDD by applying the function f to each element of each partition of this RDD. With *map()*, it is easy and quick to apply transformations to your entire dataset. Let's check an example. Imagine you want to know how many records per station we have in our RECORDS dataset:

```
>>> records_rdd = sc.textFile("/tmp/2018.csv")

>>> records_rdd.take(2)
[u'US1MISW0005,20180101,PRCP,0,,,N,',
u'US1MISW0005,20180101,SNOW,0,,,N,']

>>> def split_the_line(x):
    return x.split(',')

>>> records_identifier = records_rdd.map(lambda x: x.split(',')[0])

>>> records_identifier.take(2)
[u'US1MISW0005', u'US1MISW0005']

>>> records_identifier_map = records_identifier.map(lambda x: (x,
1))

>>> records_identifier_map.take(2)
[(u'US1MISW0005', 1), (u'US1MISW0005', 1)]
```

[Continues in next page]

42

```
>>> records_identifier_count =
records_identifier_map.reduceByKey(lambda a, b: a + b)

>>> records_identifier_count.take(2)
[(u'CA003024925', 1830), (u'US1TXLS0005', 658)]
```

First, we read our CSV file as a text file. Spark is going to take each line as a record containing one string that represents the line, for example 'US1MISW0005,20180101,PRCP,0,,,N,', and then using the function *split_the_line()*, each line is mapped to the first element (station identifier) of splitting the line per ',', and this way the line 'US1MISW0005,20180101,PRCP,0,,,N,' is mapped to 'US1MISW0005.' Then another map is applied, and each station identifier is mapped to (Identifier, 1). For example, 'US1MISW0005' is mapped to ('US1MISW0005', 1), and finally the function *reduceByKey* is used to count the number of times the station identifier appears. We will study *reduceByKey* later.

There are several variations of the *map()* function; we will study them later. Bear in mind, when you apply a *map()* to an RDD of n elements, it will generate a new RDD of n elements.

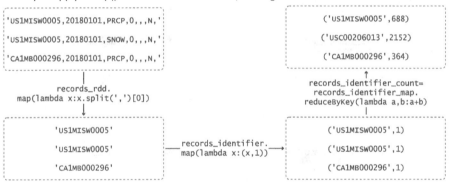

Figure 25: Map transformations

flatMap(f)

It is similar to *map()*, but with the difference that it returns a list of 0 or more elements. For example, let's count the number of times a word appears in STATION_NAME of the dataset STATIONS.

```
>>> stations_rdd = sc.textFile("/tmp/ghcnd-stations.csv")

>>> stations_rdd.count()
108082

>>> stations_rdd.take(2)
[u'ACW00011604, 17.1167, -61.7833, 10.1, ST JOHNS COOLIDGE FLD ',
u'ACW00011647, 17.1333, -61.7833, 19.2, ST JOHNS ']

>>> stations_names = stations_rdd.map(lambda line:
line.split(',')[4])

>>> stations_names.count()
108082

>>> stations_names.take(2)
[u' ST JOHNS COOLIDGE FLD ', u' ST JOHNS ']

>>> stations_names_words = stations_names.flatMap(lambda name:
name.split(' '))

>>> stations_names_words.count()
326389

>>> stations_names_words.take(2)
[u'ST', u'JOHNS']

>>> stations_names_words_map = stations_names_words.map(lambda
word: (word, 1))

>>> stations_names_words_map.count()
326389

>>> stations_names_words_map.take(2)
[(u'ST', 1), (u'JOHNS', 1)]

>>> stations_names_words_count =
stations_names_words_map.reduceByKey(lambda a, b: a +
b).sortBy(lambda (x,y): y, False)

>>> stations_names_words_count.count()
53028

>>> stations_names_words_count.take(2)
[(u'TX', 4841), (u'NE', 4665)]
```

The algorithm is simple:

- Read the file.
- Each line is divided by ',' and mapped to STATION_NAME (index 4).
- Each STATION_NAME is divided by ' ', and using *flatMap()*, a new RDD is created that contains one word per record. If you follow the counts in the code, there are 108,082 records in the RDD *station_names*, and after you apply the *flatMap()*, there are 326,389 records.
- Each word is mapped to *(word, 1)*.
- Using *reduceByKey()*, the count is performed, and finally using *sortBy()*, the counts are sorted in descending order.

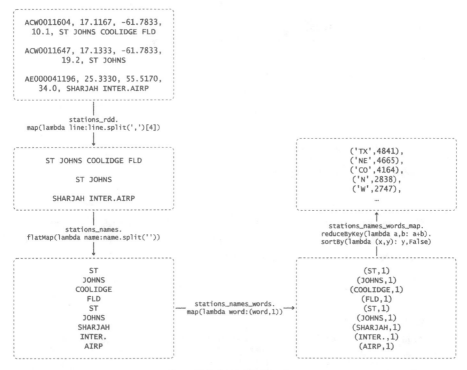

Figure 26: flatMaps transformations

filter(f)

It applies a function *f* to each element of the RDD. This function must return *true* or *false*; if the evaluation of this function returns *true*, the element is included in a new RDD. Otherwise, it will be excluded. For example, let's count the number of records in the RECORDS dataset for the STATION 'US1MISW0005'.

```
>>> records_rdd = sc.textFile("/tmp/2018.csv")

>>> records_rdd.count()
34126532

>>> records_rdd.take(3)
[u'US1MISW0005,20180101,PRCP,0,,,N,',
u'US1MISW0005,20180101,SNOW,0,,,N,']

>>> records_US1MISW0005 = records_rdd.filter(lambda line:
line.split(',')[0] == 'US1MISW0005')

>>> records_US1MISW0005.take(3)
[u'US1MISW0005,20180101,PRCP,0,,,N,',
u'US1MISW0005,20180101,SNOW,0,,,N,',
u'US1MISW0005,20180102,PRCP,0,,,N,']

>>> records_US1MISW0005.count()
88
```

In this case, we use the *filter()* function to select only the records that contain the STATION US1MISW0005; the selected records form a new RDD called records_US1MISW0005, and then the count returns 688 out of 34,126,532 records.

sortBy(f) and sortByKey()

sortBy() receives a lambda or named function and orders the elements according to this function. In the case of *sortByKey()*, it assumes the values are (key, value) pairs and orders the elements according to the key.

```
>>> stations_rdd = sc.textFile("/tmp/ghcnd-stations.csv")

>>> stations_names_words_map = stations_rdd.map(lambda line:
line.split(',')[4]).flatMap(lambda name: name.split('
')).map(lambda word: (word, 1)).reduceByKey(lambda a, b: a + b)

>>> stations_names_words_map.take(2)
[(u'CHARDZHEV', 1), (u'JOHNNY', 1)]

>>> stations_names_words_map.sortBy(lambda (x,y): y).take(2)
[(u'CHARDZHEV', 1), (u'JOHNNY', 1)]
```

[Continues in next page]

```
>>> stations_names_words_map.sortBy(lambda (x,y): y, False).take(2)
[(u'TX', 4841), (u'NE', 4665)]

>>> stations_names_words_map.sortBy(lambda (x,y): ~y,
False).take(2)
[(u'CHARDZHEV', 1), (u'JOHNNY', 1)]

>>> stations_names_words_map.sortBy(lambda (x,y): ~y).take(2)
[(u'TX', 4841), (u'NE', 4665)]

>>> stations_names_words_map.sortByKey().take(2)
[(u'A', 1), (u'B', 4)]

>>> stations_names_words_map.sortByKey(False).take(2)
[(u'Zirkel', 1), (u'ZZOR', 1)]
```

Many Transformations

There are many transformations you can apply to RDDs. You can visit the Python API page at **https://spark.apache.org/docs/latest/api/python/pyspark.html?highlight=rdd#pys park.RDD** to get a better idea of which transformations are available, and there are many more depending on the type of RDD you are using. For example, for RDDs we have:

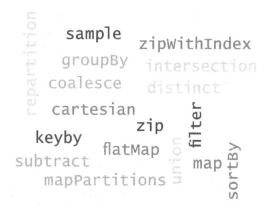

Figure 27: Transformations available in RDDs

For example, for the type PairRDD, we have the following transformations available:

Figure 28: Transformations available in PairRDDs

Actions

Transformations are what change your data, but Spark is lazy. When you define transformations or when any computation is done, to trigger the computations, you need *actions*. They indicate to Spark that it is time to start processing. In previous chapters, we used actions to bring data back to the driver, like *collect()*, take() and *saveAsTextFile()*. Some actions available in RDDs are:

variance
saveAsTextFile   takeSample
collectAsMap forEach   sum
collect first top
aggregate count   min
mean stdev   max
saveAsNewAPIHadoopDataset
saveAsSequenceFile   treeReduce

Figure 29: Actions in RDDs

Partitions

At a high level and in simple words, partitions are a bunch of data, but because we are able to take our data and divide it, partitions is one of the foundations of parallel processing in Spark. And like in any schema, partitions divide and conquer. Operating our data in partitions is way faster because we have data locality, and there is no need to move data around through the network. We have reduced operations, and we have shuffling; the performance is lower but better than without using partitions. That's why, when possible, you should group data that you will operate on together in the same partition to minimize the bandwidth usage because of it being moving data.

An important principle that we have to always keep in mind is *Data Locality*. Spark tries to work with the data that is close to the executors. Thus, when running in YARN, it tries to read HDFS blocks that are close to the executors. Also, Spark will determine the resources available and will create partitions based on how many executors it has available. You can define the number of partitions by code as we saw earlier using *repartition()* and *coalesce()*. Spark determines how to shuffle the data using a partitioner like Range or Hash partitioner.

Is it better to have more or fewer partitions? Well, it is a trade-off. More partitions means less data per partition and more and faster jobs. With more partitions, you can achieve a good level of parallelism; this is OK if you have enough worker nodes and the overhead to start a new job is not a problem. But with fewer partitions, you have more data per partition, which means larger jobs, and this is totally fine if the large chunks of data can be processed efficiently with the worker nodes you have available. The whole point is having the cluster as busy as possible with the number of partitions equal to the number of executors available. Let's check an example. We are going to define a partitioner for our data and actually partition our data using this partitioner.

```
>>> stations_rdd = sc.textFile("/tmp/ghcnd-stations.csv")

>>> stations_rdd.partitioner

>>> stations_rdd_50 = stations_rdd.repartition(50)

>>> stations_rdd_50.partitioner

>>> def rows_partitioner(row):
        return hash(row)

>>> stations_rdd = sc.textFile("/tmp/ghcnd-stations.csv")

>>> stations_rdd.partitioner

>>> stations_rdd_50 = stations_rdd.repartition(50)

>>> stations_rdd_50.partitioner
```

[Continues in next page]

```
>>> def rows_partitioner(row):
return hash(row)

>>> stations_rdd_50 = stations_rdd.partitionBy(50,
rows_partitioner)

>>> stations_rdd_50.partitioner
<pyspark.rdd.Partitioner object at 0x1086e5310>

>>> stations_rdd.saveAsTextFile('/tmp/stations_nei_partitioner')

>>> stations_rdd_50.saveAsTextFile('/tmp/stations_yei_partitioner')

>>> stations_rdd_50 = stations_rdd.partitionBy(50,
rows_partitioner)

>>> stations_rdd_50.partitioner
<pyspark.rdd.Partitioner object at 0x1086e5310>

>>> stations_rdd.saveAsTextFile('/tmp/stations_nei_partitioner')

>>> stations_rdd_50.saveAsTextFile('/tmp/stations_yei_partitioner')
```

In this example, we are using *partitionBy()*. It receives the number of desired partitions and partitioner as parameters; it will put the elements with the same key into the same partition. When defining a partition, you have to be careful with *data skew*, which is where you have some partitions with little data, while others can be so big that you might even get out-of-memory exceptions.

There is another operation we want to show you. It is called *gloom()*, and it is an action that will coalesce all rows in one partition and then convert it into an array. For example:

```
>>> for p in stations_rdd.map(lambda line:
line.split(',')[0]).glom().collect():
    print p
```

In this example, we use *gloom()* to print all the STATIONS of the elements in the RDD. We have also *mapPartitions()* and *mapPartitionsWithIndex()*. It works like a map. You specify a function, and the function receives an iterator and returns any other type. In the following example, we are going to return the total number of elements in each partition.

```
>>> stations_rdd = sc.textFile("/tmp/ghcnd-stations.csv")

>>> def count_records(iterator):
    total = 0
    for ite in iterator:
        total += 1
        yield total

>>> stations_rdd_counts = stations_rdd.mapPartitions(count_records)

>>> stations_rdd_counts.collect()
[54718, 53364]

>>> stations_rdd.count()
108082
```

The function is applied in a single pass over all the elements per partition and returned after the entire partition is processed

Sampling Data

Sampling is a functionality that might come in quite handy when working with large datasets. With sampling, you select a representative part of the population, and you work with this subset. This for sure is a lot faster than working with the entire dataset, and it is not a bad practice. For example:

```
>>> stations_rdd = sc.textFile("/tmp/ghcnd-stations.csv")

>>> stations_rdd.count()
108082

>>> stations_sample = stations_rdd.sample(False,0.1,50)

>>> stations_sample.count()
10618

>>> stations_rdd.countApprox(100, 0.95)
108082
```

Set Operations

Set theory is a branch of mathematical logic that studies sets where a set is just a collection of objects, and RDDs contain collections of objects. This means that you can apply operations like union, join, subtract, left, rightOuterJoin and more to extract information from your datasets. Let's prepare our datasets:

```
>>> stations_rdd = sc.textFile("/tmp/ghcnd-stations.csv")

>>> records_rdd = sc.textFile("/tmp/2018.csv")

>>> stations = stations_rdd.map(lambda line: line.split(","))

>>> records = records_rdd.map(lambda line: line.split(","))

>>> stations.take(3)
[ [u'ACW00011604', u' 17.1167', u' -61.7833', u' 10.1', u' ST JOHNS
COOLIDGE FLD '], [u'ACW00011647', u' 17.1333', u' -61.7833', u'
19.2', u' ST JOHNS ']]

>>> records.take(3)
[[u'US1MISW0005', u'20180101', u'PRCP', u'0', u'', u'', u'N', u''],
[u'US1MISW0005', u'20180101', u'SNOW', u'0', u'', u'', u'N', u'']]
```

If we use the transformation *union()* between both RDDs the result will be a new RDD with all the elements of both RDDs, even if they are of different types. In the following example, we are going to use UNION between RECORDS (34,126,532 rows) and STATIONS (108,082 datasets).

```
>>> records.count()
34126532

>>> stations.count()
108082

>>> stations.union(records).count()
34234614
```

If we use *join()*, it is going to show the elements that exist in both RDDs. If the RDDs are not pairRDDs, an error will be thrown. For example:

```
>>> records_data = records.map(lambda row: (row[0], row[1]+" -
"+row[2]+": "+row[3]))

>>> stations_data = stations.map(lambda row: (row[0], row[4]))

>>> records_data.take(2)
[(u'US1MISW0005', u'20180101 - PRCP: 0'), (u'US1MISW0005',
u'20180101 - SNOW: 0')]

>>> stations_data.take(2)
[ (u'ACW00011604', u' ST JOHNS COOLIDGE FLD '), (u'ACW00011647', u'
ST JOHNS ')]

>>> stations_data.join(records_data).take(2)
[(u'US1COLR0453', (u' CO BLV 1.0 S ', u'20180115 - PRCP: 3')),
(u'US1COLR0453', (u' CO BLV 1.0 S ', u'20180115 - SNOW: 5'))]

>>> stations_data.join(records_data).count()
34126532
```

In this operation, there is a lot of shuffling, so it is really expensive. Another join type is *fullOuterJoin()*. It is like the *join()* operation, but it will include None where a key doesn't appear in one RDD. One example is the station ID 'ACW00011604'; it doesn't have any record in the RECORDS dataset.

```
>>> stations_data.fullOuterJoin(records_data).count()
34195015

>>> stations_data.leftOuterJoin(records_data).count()
34195015

>>> stations_data.rightOuterJoin(records_data).count()
34126532
```

leftOuterJoin() and *rightOuterJoin()* are similar to *fullOuterJoin()*. In the left join, it uses the keys of the left RDD and includes None when the key is not found in the right RDD, and vice versa in the case of the right join. For example:

```
>>> stations_data.fullOuterJoin(records_data).count()
34195015

>>> stations_data.fullOuterJoin(records_data).filter(lambda (x,y):
x == 'ACW00011604').take(2)
[(u'ACW00011604', (u' ST JOHNS COOLIDGE FLD ', None))]
```

The final set transformation is *cartesian()*, where all elements of the left RDD are combined with the elements of the right RDD to produce an RDD with all the possible combinations.

```
>>> cartesian_stations_records =
stations_data.cartesian(records_data)

>>> cartesian_stations_records.count()
3688463831624

>>> cartesian_stations_records.take(2)
[((u'ACW00011604', u' ST JOHNS COOLIDGE FLD '), (u'US1MISW0005',
u'20180101 - PRCP: 0')), ((u'ACW00011604', u' ST JOHNS COOLIDGE FLD
'), (u'US1MISW0005', u'20180101 - SNOW: 0'))]
```

Aggregations

Aggregation is basically the act of grouping elements together, and it is the foundation of Big Data analytics. These operations are performed all the time when you want to obtain information from a dataset, like "How many of each kind do I have?" Let's check some of the aggregations available in Spark.

groupByKey()

It operates over a PairRDD; when used, it groups all the values of the elements with the same key together. In this operation, there is a lot of shuffling because data is sent over the network and collected by reduce workers. It is really inconvenient in large datasets.

```
>>> records_rdd = sc.textFile("/tmp/2018.csv")

>>> def split_the_line(x):
    return x.split(',')

>>> records = records_rdd.map(lambda line: line.split(","))

>>> records_data = records.map(lambda row: (row[0], row[1]+" -
"+row[2]+": "+row[3]))

>>> records_data.take(2)
[ (u'US1MISW0005', u'20180101 - PRCP: 0'), (u'US1MISW0005',
u'20180101 - SNOW: 0')]

>>> data_grouped = records_data.groupByKey()

>>> list(data_grouped.lookup('US1MISW0005')[0])[0:5]
[u'20180101 - PRCP: 0', u'20180101 - SNOW: 0', u'20180102 - PRCP:
0', u'20180102 - SNOW: 0', u'20180102 - SNWD: 89']

>>> len(data_grouped.lookup('US1MISW0005')[0])
688
```

In the example, records were grouped by station when a *groupByKey()* was applied. Then we looked up using the station ID 'US1MISW0005', and a subset of five elements out of 688 is shown.

reduceByKey()

This function is used in PairRDDs. It merges the values for each key using a function *f*. It is performed locally first; this reduces the amount of shuffling. After it is applied locally, the resulting values (key-value pairs) are merged globally.

```
>>> records_rdd = sc.textFile("/tmp/2018.csv")

>>> def split_the_line(x):
    return x.split(',')

>>> records = records_rdd.map(lambda line: line.split(","))

>>> records_map = records.map(lambda row: (row[0], 1))

>>> records_count = records_map.reduceByKey(lambda accum, n: accum
+ n)

>>> records_count.take(3)
[(u'USC00206013', 2152), (u'CA003024925', 1830), (u'US1TXLS0005',
658)]

>>> stations_rdd = sc.textFile("/tmp/ghcnd-stations.csv")

>>> stations = stations_rdd.map(lambda line: line.split(","))

>>> stations_data = stations.map(lambda row: (row[0], row[4]))

>>> stations_data.innerJoin(records_count).take(3)
[(u'US1COLR0453', (u' CO BLV 1.0 S ', 132)), (u'US1INAL0053', (u'
IN FORT WAYNE 5.5 N ', 564)), (u'USC00455224', (u' WA MCMILLIN RSVR
', 1062))]
```

If *reduceByKey()* or *groupByKey()* use the same operation, it will produce the same results.

Each record was mapped to a tuple with format *(STATION, 1)*, and then *reduceByKey()* was used to sum all values from the tuples grouped by key, and the result is an RDD that contains tuples of the form *(STATION, number of records)*. Inspecting the resulting RDD, we can say that station USC00206013 has 2,152 records in the dataset. Finally, we use the *join* to associate the name of the station with the number of records that exist for that station in the dataset.

aggregateByKey()

It is like *reduceByKey()* except that it takes an initial value, and it receives two functions, one combining function (it applies to each partition) and one merging function (it applies globally). The number of partitions and initial value can affect the order and the results

Continuing with the previous example:

```
>>> records_map.aggregateByKey(0,lambda accum, n: accum + n, lambda
accun1, accun2: accun1+accun2).take(2)
[(u'USC00206013', 2152), (u'CA003024925', 1830)]

>>> records_map.repartition(1).aggregateByKey(0,lambda accum, n:
accum + n, lambda accun1, accun2: accun1+accun2).take(2)
[(u'US1ILFL0011', 574), (u'USS0006H19S', 2555)]

>>> records_map.repartition(8).aggregateByKey(10,lambda accum, n:
accum + n, lambda accun1, accun2: accun1+accun2).take(2)
[(u'USC00477015', 363), (u'GME00122962', 1387)]

>>> records_map.repartition(5).aggregateByKey(10,lambda accum, n:
accum + n, lambda accun1, accun2: accun1+accun2).take(2)
[(u'US1COGF0002', 607), (u'ASN00090077', 413)]

>>> records_map.repartition(3).aggregateByKey(10,lambda accum, n:
accum + n, lambda accun1, accun2: accun1+accun2).take(2)
[(u'US1ILFL0011', 604), (u'US1INHS0008', 507)]
```

combineByKey()

It operates over PairRDDs; basically, it is defined as:

```
combineByKey(createCombiner, mergeValue, mergeCombiners)
```

The first function is *createCombiner,* and it is going to be used to create the initial value. For example, imagine that we have the following data:

```
data = [("Z", 12), ("A", 1), ("R", 3), ("A", 10), ("C", 20),
("R", 3), ("A", 5), ("B", 8), ("R", 12) ]
rdd1 = sc.parallelize( data )
```

Imagine the following partitions:

Partition 1	Partition 2
("Z", 12)	("R", 3)
("A", 1)	("A", 5)
("R", 3)	("B", 8)
("A", 10)	("R", 12)
("C", 20)	

And we are going to use the function as a combiner:

```
rdd1.map(lambda keyPair: (keyPair, 1)).collect()
```

It is going to create as initial value:

Partition 1	Partition 2
"Z" -> (12,1)	"R" -> (3,1)
"A" -> (1,1)	"A" -> (5,1)
"R" -> (3,1)	"B" -> (8,1)
"A" -> (10,1)	"R" -> (12,1)
"C" -> (20,1)	

The *mergeValue* function will reduce each partition; for example, if we use the following function:

```
lambda x, value: (x[0] + value, x[1] + 1)
```

It will produce the following values:

Partition 1	Partition 2
"Z" -> (12,1)	"R" -> (3,1)
"A" -> (11,2) (mergeValue used with	"A" -> (5,1)
elements "A" -> (1,1) and "A" -> (10,1))	
"R" -> (3,1)	"B" -> (8,1)
"C" -> (20,1)	"R" -> (12,1)

Then the *mergeCombiners* will combine values of combiners with the same key. For example, we can use the function:

```
lambda x, y: (x[0] + y[0], x[1] + y[1])
```

The result:

Collect()
"Z" -> (12,1)
"A" -> (16,3)
"R" -> (18,3)
"C" -> (20,1)
"B" -> (8,1)

The following example is going to calculate the average VALUE of each OBSERVATION for each STATION. For this example, we are going to read the dataset, and then each line is divided by ',', and each record is going to be mapped to ('STATION-OBSERVATION', float(VALUE)). For example, [u'US1MISW0005', u'20180101', u'PRCP', u'0', u'', u'', u'N', u''] is going to be mapped to (u'US1MISW0005- PRCP', 0.0), and when combine by key is applied, the following value is going to be produced: ('STATION-OBSERVATION',(SUM VALUES, COUNT VALUES)). For example, the output for 'US1MISW0005- PRCP' is [(u'US1MISW0005-PRCP', (8643.0, 339))]. Finally, we transform each result to (STATION, OBSERVATION, SUM VALUES/COUNT VALUES), and the following result is obtained for the STATION 'US1MISW0005':

[(u'US1MISW0005', u'SNWD', 54.39316239316239), (u'US1MISW0005', u'PRCP', 25.495575221238937), (u'US1MISW0005', u'WESF', 0.0), (u'US1MISW0005', u'SNOW', 6.378260869565217)]

```
>>> records_rdd = sc.textFile("/tmp/2018.csv")

>>> records = records_rdd.map(lambda line: line.split(","))

>>> records.take(2)
[[u'US1MISW0005', u'20180101', u'PRCP', u'0', u'', u'', u'N', u''],
[u'US1MISW0005', u'20180101', u'SNOW', u'0', u'', u'', u'N', u'']]

>>> records_map = records.map(lambda row: (row[0]+"-"+row[2],
float(row[3])))

>>> records_map.take(2)
[(u'US1MISW0005-PRCP', 0.0), (u'US1MISW0005-SNOW', 0.0)]

>>> records_totals = records_map.combineByKey(lambda value: (value,
1),lambda x, value: (x[0] + value, x[1] + 1),lambda x, y: (x[0] +
y[0], x[1] + y[1]))

>>> records_totals.take(2)
[(u'US1NCIR0021-PRCP', (15620.0, 327)), (u'ASN00004026-PRCP',
(4073.0, 151))]

>>> records_avg = records_totals.map(lambda row: (row[0].split('-
')[0],row[0].split('-')[1], row[1][0]/row[1][1]))
```

[Continues in next page]

```
>>> records_avg.take(2)
[(u'US1NCIR0021', u'PRCP', 47.76758409785933), (u'ASN00004026',
u'PRCP', 26.973509933774835)]

>>> records_avg.filter(lambda row: row[0] ==
'US1MISW0005').collect()
[(u'US1MISW0005', u'SNWD', 54.39316239316239), (u'US1MISW0005',
u'PRCP', 25.495575221238937), (u'US1MISW0005', u'WESF', 0.0),
(u'US1MISW0005', u'SNOW', 6.378260869565217)]
```

countByKey()

It returns a map with the keys and count of occurrences. For example:

```
>>> records_rdd = sc.textFile("/tmp/2018.csv")

>>> records = records_rdd.map(lambda line: line.split(","))

>>> records_map = records.map(lambda row: (row[0], row))

>>> records_map.take(3)
[(u'US1MISW0005', [u'US1MISW0005', u'20180101', u'PRCP', u'0', u'',
u'', u'N', u'']), (u'US1MISW0005', [u'US1MISW0005', u'20180101',
u'SNOW', u'0', u'', u'', u'N', u''])]

>>> records_count = records_map.countByKey()

>>> records_count['US1MISW0005']
688
```

histogram() – Grouping Data Into Buckets

A histogram is a powerful visualization tool. It helps to perform statistical data exploration. To define a histogram, it is a diagram consisting of rectangles whose area is proportional to the frequency of a variable and whose width is equal to the class interval.

Probably the hardest part is to get the buckets of data, especially with large datasets, but Spark makes it easy to group data into buckets with the *histogram()* function.

For the *histogram()* function, you can specify the number of buckets you want. In this case, the domain of the data will be split equally, or you can specify the buckets and their sizes. For example:

```
>>> histRDD = sc.paralelize(range(997))

>>> histRDD.take(10)
[0, 1, 2, 3, 4, 5, 6, 7, 8, 9]

>>> histRDD.histogram(3) # number of buckets
([0, 332, 664, 996], [332, 332, 333])

>>> histRDD.histogram(8)
([0.0, 124.5, 249.0, 373.5, 498.0, 622.5, 747.0, 871.5, 996], [125, 124, 125, 124, 125, 124, 125, 125])

>>> histRDD.histogram([0,100,500,711,1000]) # specify buckets
([0, 100, 500, 711, 1000], [100, 400, 211, 286])

>>> histWordsRDD = sc.parallelize(["abigail","bronwen", "alice", "clementine", "cora", "daisy"])

>>> histWordsRDD.histogram(["a","b","c"])
(['a', 'b', 'c'], [2, 1])

>>> histWordsRDD.histogram(["a","b","c","d"])
(['a', 'b', 'c', 'd'], [2, 1, 2])

>>> histWordsRDD.histogram(["a","b","c","d","f"])
(['a', 'b', 'c', 'd', 'f'], [2, 1, 2, 1])

>>> histWordsRDD.histogram(["a","b","c","d","f","g"])
(['a', 'b', 'c', 'd', 'f', 'g'], [2, 1, 2, 1, 0])
```

Cache and Data Persistence

Spark can perform caching of intermediate results, and this can help on expensive operations to avoid recomputing when a node fails. For example, let's check the following code from the *combineByKey()* example:

```
>>> records_rdd = sc.textFile("/tmp/2018.csv")

>>> records = records_rdd.map(lambda line: line.split(","))

>>> records_map = records.map(lambda row: (row[0]+"-"+row[2], float(row[3])))
```

[Continues in next page]

```
>>> records_totals = records_map.combineByKey(lambda value: (value,
1),lambda x, value: (x[0] + value, x[1] + 1),lambda x, y: (x[0] +
y[0], x[1] + y[1]))

>>> records_avg = records_totals.map(lambda row: (row[0].split('-
')[0],row[0].split('-')[1], row[1][0]/row[1][1]))

>>> records_avg.filter(lambda row: row[0] ==
'US1MISW0005').collect()
[(u'US1MISW0005', u'SNWD', 54.39316239316239), (u'US1MISW0005',
u'PRCP', 25.495575221238937), (u'US1MISW0005', u'WESF', 0.0),
(u'US1MISW0005', u'SNOW', 6.378260869565217)]

>>> records_avg.filter(lambda row: row[0] ==
'ASN00015643').collect()
[(u'ASN00015643', u'TMAX', 323.958904109589), (u'ASN00015643',
u'TMIN', 142.07988980716254), (u'ASN00015643', u'PRCP'
3.016759776536313)]
```

In this example, we performed more than one *action* over the RDD *records_avg*. Remember that Spark is lazy; this means when you execute the action, it calculates the lineage graph and calculates the RDD *records_avg* (and its parents up to *records_rdd*). We called two *filter()* actions over *records_avg,* so for example, .map(lambda row: (row[0].split('-')[0],row[0].split('-')[1],   row[1][0]/row[1][1])) is calculated two times. We can avoid that by using *cache()*, which tells Spark that once *records_avg* is calculated, to save the results for future use. The code using cache looks like this:

```
>>> records_rdd = sc.textFile("/tmp/2018.csv")

>>> records = records_rdd.map(lambda line: line.split(","))

>>> records_map = records.map(lambda row: (row[0]+"-"+row[2],
float(row[3])))

>>> records_totals = records_map.combineByKey(lambda value: (value,
1),lambda x, value: (x[0] + value, x[1] + 1),lambda x, y: (x[0] +
y[0], x[1] + y[1]))

>>> records_avg = records_totals.map(lambda row: (row[0].split('-
')[0],row[0].split('-')[1], row[1][0]/row[1][1]))

>>> records_avg.cache()

>>> records_avg.filter(lambda row: row[0] ==
'US1MISW0005').collect()
[(u'US1MISW0005', u'SNWD', 54.39316239316239), (u'US1MISW0005',
u'PRCP', 25.495575221238937), (u'US1MISW0005', u'WESF', 0.0),
(u'US1MISW0005', u'SNOW', 6.378260869565217)]
```

[Continues in next page]

```
>>> records_avg.filter(lambda row: row[0] ==
'ASN00015643').collect()
[(u'ASN00015643', u'TMAX', 323.958904109589), (u'ASN00015643',
u'TMIN', 142.07988980716254), (u'ASN00015643', u'PRCP',
3.016759776536313)]
```

Since *cache()* breaks the lineage because Spark saves the RDD and it is not recalculated anymore, it doesn't depend on its parents.

Now, imagine a scenario where the same job is executed twice. Maybe the intermediate results have been removed from the cache. Persist does the magic; it saves the intermediate results in disk and uses it later.

Shared Variables

Each executor has a copy of the variables; modifications to the variable cannot be replicated, and there is no propagation back to the driver. Variables are part of the closure. If there is a need of shared information between the controller and executors, Spark provides accumulators and broadcast variables.

A *broadcast variable* is a read-only variable; it is immutable and kept in memory. It is distributed across all the executors in the cluster, and it is not modified in transit. For example, you can broadcast a lookup table.

```
>>> broadCastRDD = sc.parallelize(range(500))

>>> modValue = 10 # local variable

>>> modValueBroadCast =sc.broadcast(modValue)

>>> broadCastRDD.map(lambda x: x%modValueBroadCast.value).take(2)
[0, 1]
```

With *accumulators*, a variable is defined that can be "added"; through an associative and commutative operation, they are written back to the driver. For example:

```
>>> accRDD = sc.parallelize(range(500))

>>> accumNum =sc.accumulator(0)

>>> def add_item(item):
       accumNum.add(item)

>>> accRDD.foreach(add_item)

>>> accumNum.value
124750

>>> accRDD.sum()
124750
```

6 Data Frames and Spark SQL

Why do we need to learn another API if we just learned RDDs? Even though we could most likely do anything we wanted with our data using RDDs, the higher-level API allows us to become proficient with Spark quicker. This is especially true if you have a background in relational databases. Since a DataFrame is equivalent to a table, we will learn how we can use them to more easily model and work with our data, including schemas, converting RDDs into DataFrames and Datasets.

Structured Query Language or SQL is considered the lingua franca for data analysis. Around the world there are millions of developers, business developers and other users who are well trained and feel comfortable working with SQL. SQL has been popular for many years; it is easy to learn, understand and use, and it is supported by many applications.

Spark SQL is a module for structured data processing. The most important added benefit is that you get a schema, something that we don't have with an RDD. A schema gives to Spark more information on the data that is being processed. For this reason Spark can perform more optimizations in the core engine. With the schema (data type and name), you can query your data issuing SQL queries. It can work with any data source that is compatible with Spark.

The other abstraction we have is called DataFrame, which is a distributed collection of Row objects. A Row is an object that contains your data, and you can access each column. From version 2.0, the DataFrame is a special case of DataSet, namely DataSet of Row. You can think of DataFrame as a database table with rows and columns, with a known schema. Using DataFrames, you can work with structured and unstructured data. Also, you can go back and forth between DataFrames and RDDs. There may be cases where it is better to use RDDs instead of DataFrames, so you can take your DataFrame and convert it to an RDD, perform operations and generate back a DataFrame.

Let's understand what happens when you run a query in Spark:

Figure 30

- You can choose between SQL Query or DataFrame; you can achieve the same result with either of them.
- It is converted to an unresolved logical plan. Remember, Spark is lazy; there are attributes or relationships that haven't been created.
- The catalog (which knows all existing entities) is used to complete missing information.
- A logical plan is generated.
- Several optimizations are applied to the logical plan (it is SQL; there is a lot to optimize).
- A new optimized logical plan is generated.
- Several physical plans are generated (how it is going to be executed in the cluster).
- A cost model is used to decide which Physical Plan is optimal.
- At the end, everything is RDDs. The code is generated and executed in the cluster.

Spark Session

Earlier, we learned about SparkSession and how it:
- Is the entry point to use SparkSQL and DataFrames.
- An abstraction that combines SparkContext and HiveContext.
- Allows access to SparkContext in case you need or want to work with RDDs.

This is how we create it:

```
from pyspark import SparkConf, SparkSession

spark = SparkSession.builder.master("yarn").appName("Test App")
        .config("spark.submit.deployMode", "".
    .config("spark.executor.memory", "2g").getOrCreate()
```

We you need to work with Spark using PySpark (REPL), the SparkSession is created for you, but if you are creating contained applications (those that will be submitted to Spark Cluster), you have to create it. One interesting characteristic of SparkSession is that you can have multiple sessions at the same time; if you remember from our previous chapters, in the case of SparkContext, you can have only one of them. This is how you can create a second SparkSession:

```
from pyspark import SparkConf, SparkSession

spark = SparkSession.builder.master("yarn").appName("Test App")
        .config("spark.submit.deployMode", "").
    .config("spark.executor.memory", "2g").getOrCreate()

spark_two = spark.newSession()
```

Each SparkSession will have independent SQLConf, UDFS and registered temporary views, and it will share the same SparkContext and table cache.

Creating and Loading DataFrames

There are multiple ways of getting a DataFrame; you can create DataFrames from data in memory, or you can load them from storage.

If you remember, in previous chapters, we used the function *parallelize()* to pass lists of data and generate RDDs. Well, we have a similar way to create DataFrames. We can use the function *CreateDataFrame()* to pass a list of data or a Panda DataFrame to generate a Spark DataFrame. For example:

```
data  = spark.createDataFrame([("Z", 12), ("A", 1), ("R", 3), ("A",
10), ("C", 20), ("R", 3), ("A", 5), ("B", 8), ("R", 12)])

>>> data.collect()
[Row(_1=u'Z', _2=12), Row(_1=u'A', _2=1), Row(_1=u'R', _2=3),
Row(_1=u'A', _2=10), Row(_1=u'C', _2=20), Row(_1=u'R', _2=3),
Row(_1=u'A', _2=5), Row(_1=u'B', _2=8), Row(_1=u'R', _2=12)]
```

You may have noticed that you can still call the function *collect()*, but its output is a little bit different than when you call the RDD method *collect()*. Each row of data is an object of type Row, which is the building block of the DataFrame. There are several object types you can use to generate a DataFrame, for example a dictionary.

```
>>> data_dic = spark.createDataFrame({("Z", 12), ("A", 1), ("R",
3), ("S", 10), ("C", 20), ("M", 3), ("O", 5), ("P", 8), ("Q", 12)})

>>> data_dic.collect()
[Row(_1=u'A', _2=1), Row(_1=u'P', _2=8), Row(_1=u'O', _2=5),
Row(_1=u'Z', _2=12), Row(_1=u'C', _2=20), Row(_1=u'R', _2=3),
Row(_1=u'Q', _2=12), Row(_1=u'M', _2=3), Row(_1=u's', _2=10)]
```

We can also create a DataFrame with a list of Row objects, for example:

```
>>> from pyspark.sql import Row

>>> data_list_rows = spark.createDataFrame([Row("Z", 12), Row("A",
1), Row("R", 3), Row("S", 10), Row("C", 20), Row("M", 3), Row("O",
5), Row("P", 8), Row("Q", 12)])

>>> data_list_rows.collect()
[Row(_1=u'Z', _2=12), Row(_1=u'A', _2=1), Row(_1=u'R', _2=3),
Row(_1=u'S', _2=10), Row(_1=u'C', _2=20), Row(_1=u'M', _2=3),
Row(_1=u'O', _2=5), Row(_1=u'P', _2=8), Row(_1=u'Q', _2=12)]

>>> data_list_rows.take(2)
[Row(_1=u'Z', _2=12), Row(_1=u'A', _2=1)]

>>> data_list_rows.show()
+----+----+
| _1 | _2 |
+----+----+
| Z  | 12 |
.
.
.
| Q  | 12.|
+----+----+

>>> data_list_rows.show(2)
+----+----+
| _1 | _2 |
+----+----+
| Z  | 12 |
| A  | 1  |
+----+----+
only showing top 2 rows

>>> data_list_rows.limit(1).show()
+---+---+
| _1| _2|
+---+---+
| Z | 12|
+---+---+

>>> data_list_rows.first()
Row(_1=u'Z', _2=12)

>>> data_list_rows.head()
Row(_1=u'Z', _2=12)

>>> data_list_rows.sample(False, .6, 42).collect()
[Row(_1=u'R', _2=3), Row(_1=u'S', _2=10), Row(_1=u'C', _2=20),
Row(_1=u'M', _2=3), Row(_1=u'O', _2=5), Row(_1=u'Q', _2=12)]
```

A *Row* object represents a row of data in the DataFrame. Each *Row* object is a container with some additional attributes; for instance, we have named columns. We can use several *actions* to retrieve data back to the driver, for example, *take(), limit(), head(), first(), sample or show()*. By the way, *show()* displays the information very nicely.

We can also add nice column names to our DataFrames. For example, we are going to add named columns to our DataFrame to stop using the names _1 and _2.

```
>>> data_nice_names = data.toDF("Character", "Count")

>>> data_nice_names.show()
+-----------+-----------+
|Character  |Count      |
+-----------+-----------+
|   Z       |   12      |
|   A       |   1       |
|   R       |   3       |
|   A       |   10      |
|   C       |   20      |
|   R       |   3       |
|   A       |   5       |
|   B       |   8       |
|   R       |   12.     |
+-----------+-----------+
```

You will soon experience how much easier it is to work with SparkSQL and DataFrames. There are cases where the flexibility offered by the RDD is better to resolve a problem, so we are going to learn how to convert from RDDs to DataFrames and vice versa.

```
>>> dataRDD = sc.parallelize([("z", 12), ("A", 1), ("R", 3)])

>>> dataRDD
ParallelCollectionRDD[52] at parallelize at PythonRDD.scala:489

>>> dataRDDToDF = dataRDD.toDF()

>>> dataRDDToDF
DataFrame[_1: string, _2: bigint]

>>> dataRDDCreate = spark.createDataFrame(dataRDD)

>>> dataRDDCreate
DataFrame[_1: string, _2: bigint]

>>> dataRDDToDF.show(1)
+---+---+
| _1| _2|
+---+---+
|  z| 12|
+---+---+
only showing top 1 row
```

[Continues in next page]

```
>>> dataRDDCreate.show(1)
+---+---+
| _1| _2|
+---+---+
|  z| 12|
+---+---+
only showing top 1 row
```

As you can see, there are two ways of creating a DataFrame from an RDD: *toDF()* and *createDataFrame()*.

Both of them have the same result, but there is a small difference: *toDF()* infers the schema, while with *createDataFrame()*, you may need to specify the schema for your data.

Loading DataFrames

There is a component called DataFrameReader, which is the class used to load data from an external data source, and it is accessible using SparkSession. There are many supported formats natively as well as multiple connectors available. You can define your custom data formats and extend DataFrameReader.

For example, lets load the data from the RECORDS dataset from NOOA.

```
>>> recordsDF=spark.read.text ('/tmp/2018.csv')

>>> recordsDF.show(5)
+--------------------+
|               value|
+--------------------+
|STATION,DATE,OBSE...|
|US1MISW0005,20180...|
|US1MISW0005,20180...|
|CA1MB000296,20180...|
|ASN00015643,20180...|
+--------------------+
only showing top 5 rows

>>> recordsDF.printSchema()
root
 |-- value: string (nullable = true)
```

As we can see, Spark didn't recognize any schema and just tried to handle everything as a huge string. In this particular case, we specified the format using the *function .format('text')*. There is another way to do it; just specify *.text()*. For example:

```
>>> recordsDF=spark.read.text ('/tmp/2018.csv')
```

[Continues in next page]

68

```
>>> recordsDF.show(5)
+----------------------+
| value                |
+----------------------+
|STATION,DATE,OBSE...  |
|US1MISW0005,20180...  |
|US1MISW0005,20180...  |
|CA1MB000296,20180...  |
|ASN00015643,20180...  |
+----------------------+
only showing top 5 rows

>>> recordsDF.printSchema()
root
     |-- value: string (nullable = true)
```

As we are working with a CSV file, we can try to load the file using this format. Let's try to do it.

```
>>> recordsDF=spark.read.csv('/tmp/2018.csv')

>>> recordsDF.printSchema()
root
     |-- _c0: string (nullable = true)
     |-- _c1: string (nullable = true)
     |-- _c2: string (nullable = true)
     |-- _c3: string (nullable = true)
     |-- _c4: string (nullable = true)
     |-- _c5: string (nullable = true)
     |-- _c6: string (nullable = true)
     |-- _c7: string (nullable = true)
```

After we specify the format type, we can show that our data is divided into columns and Spark understood we have columnar data. Something interesting is that Spark is not understanding we have column names and some kind of schema. For example, it recognized all columns as String. Depending on the data format we are using, there are several options we can pass. For example, in the case of CSV, you can specify the separator, maximum number of chars per column, max columns and what to do on null values, just to mention a few.

```
>>> recordsDF=spark.read.csv('/tmp/2018.csv', inferSchema=True)

                        [Continues in next page]
```

```
>>> recordsDF.printSchema()
root
     |-- _c0: string (nullable = true)
     |-- _c1: string (nullable = true)
     |-- _c2: string (nullable = true)
     |-- _c3: string (nullable = true)
     |-- _c4: string (nullable = true)
     |-- _c5: string (nullable = true)
     |-- _c6: string (nullable = true)
     |-- _c7: string (nullable = true)

>>> stationsDF=spark.read.csv('/tmp/ghcnd-
stations.csv',inferSchema=True)

>>> stationsDF.printSchema()
root
     |-- _c0: string (nullable = true)
     |-- _c1: string (nullable = true)
     |-- _c2: string (nullable = true)
     |-- _c3: string (nullable = true)
     |-- _c4: string (nullable = true)
```

As you can see, we obtained the same result. The problem is that we have the header inside the file, and Spark is going to recognize the column type that best fits the data present in all the rows of the file.

The good news is that you have plenty of options, and one of them is that we can tell Spark that there is a Header in the file. For example:

```
>>> recordsDF=spark.read.csv('/tmp/2018.csv',inferSchema=True,
header=True)

>>> recordsDF.printSchema()
root
     |-- STATION: string (nullable = true)
     |-- DATE: integer (nullable = true)
     |-- OBSERVATION: string (nullable = true)
     |-- VALUE: integer (nullable = true)
     |-- MF: string (nullable = true)
     |-- QF: string (nullable = true)
     |-- SF: string (nullable = true)
     |-- TIME: integer (nullable = true)

>>> stationsDF=spark.read.csv('/tmp/ghcnd-
stations.csv',inferSchema=True, header=True)

>>> stationsDF.printSchema()
root
     |-- STATION: string (nullable = true)
     |-- LATITUDE: double (nullable = true)
     |-- LONGITUDE: double (nullable = true)
     |-- ELEVATION: double (nullable = true)
     |-- STATION_NAME: string (nullable = true)
```

That looks better, right? It is because Spark read the data and inspected part of the rows to infer the type of the data, and also as we specified that we have a header, Spark recognized the friendly column names.

In the previous example, we passed the options inferSchema and header as parameters to the function CSV, but there are other ways to do it. You can use the function *option()*. For example:

```
>>> recordsDF=spark.read.option('inferSchema', 'true').option(
'header', 'true').csv('/tmp/2018.csv')

>>> recordsDF.printSchema()
root
    |-- STATION: string (nullable = true)
    |-- DATE: integer (nullable = true)
    |-- OBSERVATION: string (nullable = true)
    |-- VALUE: integer (nullable = true)
    |-- MF: string (nullable = true)
    |-- QF: string (nullable = true)
    |-- SF: string (nullable = true)
    |-- TIME: integer (nullable = true)
```

Also, you can use the function *options();* you can pass several options to Spark to modify the way data is read.

Sometimes, inferSchema doesn't work as expected. This is because we can have corrupted data in our file, there is a mistake in the data or Spark is not smart enough to recognize the data type. We can create custom schemas by using *StructType* and *StructField* and then pass the schema to Spark. For example:

```
>>> from pyspark.sql.types import *

>>> newSchema=StructType([
    StructField("STATION", StringType()),
    StructField("DATE", TimestampType()),
    StructField("OBSERVATION", StringType()),
    StructField("VALUE", DoubleType()),
    StructField("MF", StringType()),
    StructField("QF", StringType()),
    StructField("SF", StringType()),
    StructField("TIME", IntegerType())])

>>> recordsDF=spark.read.schema(newSchema).csv('/tmp/2018.csv',
header=True)
```

[Continues in next page]

71

```
>>> recordsDF.printSchema()
root
     |-- STATION: string (nullable = true)
     |-- DATE: timestamp (nullable = true)
     |-- OBSERVATION: string (nullable = true)
     |-- VALUE: double (nullable = true)
     |-- MF: string (nullable = true)
     |-- QF: string (nullable = true)
     |-- SF: string (nullable = true)
     |-- TIME: integer (nullable = true)

>>> recordsDF.schema
StructType(List(StructField(STATION,StringType,true),StructField(DA
TE,TimestampType,true),StructField(OBSERVATION,StringType,true),Str
uctField(VALUE,DoubleType,true),StructField(MF,StringType,true),Str
uctField(QF,StringType,true),StructField(SF,StringType,true),Struct
Field(TIME,IntegerType,true)))

>>> recordsDF.dtypes [('STATION', 'string'), ('DATE', 'timestamp'),
('OBSERVATION', 'string'), ('VALUE', 'double'), ('MF', 'string'),
('QF', 'string'), ('SF', 'string'), ('TIME', 'int')]

>>> recordsDF.columns
['STATION', 'DATE', 'OBSERVATION', 'VALUE', 'MF', 'QF', 'SF',
'TIME']
```

Parquet

Parquet is a columnar file format originally created by Cloudera and Twitter. It is too efficient; it has features like reading only the columns used in the query. It is supported by many Big Data systems including Spark, MapReduce, Hive, Pig and Impala, just to name a few, and it is the default format when working with the higher level Spark API.

Some advantages of Parquet are:

- It preserves the original schema; it is actually packaged in the same file.
- It optimizes data storage.
- It has really good performance, especially because of its optimized data storage layer.
- It works especially well with large amounts of data.

Let's create a Parquet file. For this purpose, we are going to read the CSV file with our data, and after that we are going to save it as a Parquet.

```
>>> recordsDF=spark.read.csv('/tmp/2018.csv',inferSchema=True,
header=True)

>>> recordsDF.printSchema()
root
    |-- STATION: string (nullable = true)
    |-- DATE: integer (nullable = true)
    |-- OBSERVATION: string (nullable = true)
    |-- VALUE: integer (nullable = true)
    |-- MF: string (nullable = true)
    |-- QF: string (nullable = true)
    |-- SF: string (nullable = true)
    |-- TIME: integer (nullable = true)

>>> recordsDF.count()
34126531

>>> recordsDF.write.parquet('/tmp/2018.parquet')
```

Now let's check the final files:

```
$ ls -lh /tmp/2018.csv
-rw-r--r--@ 1 user group 1.1G Apr 6 11:03 /tmp/2018.csv

$ du -sh /tmp/2018.parquet/
121M /tmp/2018.parquet/

$ ls -l /tmp/2018.parquet/
total 244864
-rw-r--r-- 1 user group 0 Apr 7 14:05 _SUCCESS
-rw-r--r-- 1 user group 13849519 Apr 7 14:05 part-00000-a0f5aa82-
9cf3-4576-8e85-ca68ed65cb4a-c000.snappy.parquet
-rw-r--r-- 1 user group 13836451 Apr 7 14:05 part-00001-a0f5aa82-
9cf3-4576-8e85-ca68ed65cb4a-c000.snappy.parquet
-rw-r--r-- 1 user group 13712146 Apr 7 14:05 part-00002-a0f5aa82-
9cf3-4576-8e85-ca68ed65cb4a-c000.snappy.parquet
-rw-r--r-- 1 user group 13287230 Apr 7 14:05 part-00003-a0f5aa82-
9cf3-4576-8e85-ca68ed65cb4a-c000.snappy.parquet
-rw-r--r-- 1 user group 13229535 Apr 7 14:05 part-00004-a0f5aa82-
9cf3-4576-8e85-ca68ed65cb4a-c000.snappy.parquet
-rw-r--r-- 1 user group 13300210 Apr 7 14:05 part-00005-a0f5aa82-
9cf3-4576-8e85-ca68ed65cb4a-c000.snappy.parquet
-rw-r--r-- 1 user group 13397902 Apr 7 14:05 part-00006-a0f5aa82-
9cf3-4576-8e85-ca68ed65cb4a-c000.snappy.parquet
-rw-r--r-- 1 user group 13431769 Apr 7 14:05 part-00007-a0f5aa82-
9cf3-4576-8e85-ca68ed65cb4a-c000.snappy.parquet
-rw-r--r-- 1 user group 12510621 Apr 7 14:05 part-00008-a0f5aa82-
9cf3-4576-8e85-ca68ed65cb4a-c000.snappy.parquet
```

As you can see, the original CSV file was about 1.1GB, and the new Parquet file is just 121MB. Now let's read the file and verify we have the same amount of data and schema.

```
>>> recordsDF=spark.read.parquet('/tmp/2018.parquet')

>>> recordsDF.printSchema()
root
    |-- STATION: string (nullable = true)
    |-- DATE: integer (nullable = true)
    |-- OBSERVATION: string (nullable = true)
    |-- VALUE: integer (nullable = true)
    |-- MF: string (nullable = true)
    |-- QF: string (nullable = true)
    |-- SF: string (nullable = true)
    |-- TIME: integer (nullable = true)

>>> recordsDF.count()
34126531
```

That's great! We have the same amount of data with less storage.

JSON

Let's try to read and write JSON files. In the same way we did with Parquet, we are going to read the CSV file, write the JSON, open the file and verify the file format, and then we are going to read it.

```
>>> recordsDF=spark.read.csv('/tmp/2018.csv',inferSchema=True,
header=True)

>>> recordsDF.count()
34126531

>>> recordsDF.printSchema()
root
    |-- STATION: string (nullable = true)
    |-- DATE: integer (nullable = true)
    |-- OBSERVATION: string (nullable = true)
    |-- VALUE: integer (nullable = true)
    |-- MF: string (nullable = true)
    |-- QF: string (nullable = true)
    |-- SF: string (nullable = true)
    |-- TIME: integer (nullable = true)

>>> recordsDF.write.json('/tmp/2018.json')

>>> recordsJSON=spark.read.json('/tmp/2018.json')
```

[Continues in next page]

```
>>> recordsJSON.count()
34126531

>>> recordsJSON.printSchema()
root
     |-- DATE: long (nullable = true)
     |-- MF: string (nullable = true)
     |-- OBSERVATION: string (nullable = true)
     |-- QF: string (nullable = true)
     |-- SF: string (nullable = true)
     |-- STATION: string (nullable = true)
     |-- TIME: long (nullable = true)
     |-- VALUE: long (nullable = true)
```

As you can see, we have the same data, and the schema changed a little bit. It improved the accuracy of the recognized data type for the columns VALUE, DATE and TIME. JSON is a text-based file format, and it requires around 2.2GB to store the dataset. Let's see what the file looks like:

```
{
"STATION": "RSM00028214",
"DATE": 20180321,
"OBSERVATION": "TMIN",
"VALUE": -115,
"SF": "S"
}
{
"STATION": "RSM00028214",
"DATE": 20180321,
"OBSERVATION": "PRCP",
"VALUE": 0,
"MF": "B",
"SF": "S"
}
```

Row, Columns, Expressions and Operators

Our DataFrame is conceptually a database table, which means that we have *rows* of data, and each *row* has named columns with a value. But is important to mention that Spark does not simply store values, which is what commonly happens in relational databases; something different happens: It contains an *expression* that is applied to every *row*.

A *catalyst expression*, to use an accurate term, produces a value per *row* for each *column*. It can be based on a value, function or operation. We will see *expressions* in action in a few minutes; be patient.

Referring columns is very important. Whenever you want to refer to a particular column, there are a few different ways to do it:

- **Canonical Notation:** In this notation, you specify the column name just like you use dictionaries with brackets. One advantage of this notation is that you can specify the column name at runtime.
- *col()* **function**
- **Dot Notation:** You specify directly the name of the column. It is case sensitive.

```
>>> recordsDF=spark.read.csv('/tmp/2018.csv',inferSchema=True,
header=True)

>>> recordsDF.STATION
Column<STATION>

>>> recordsDF["STATION"]
Column<STATION>
```

And now let's use the notations to specify which columns we want to return. For instance:

```
>>> from pyspark.sql.functions import concat, col, lit

>>> recordsDF=spark.read.csv('/tmp/2018.csv',inferSchema=True,
header=True)

>>> recordsDF.select(recordsDF.STATION).show(2)
+--------------------+
| STATION            |
+--------------------+
|US1MISW0005         |
|US1MISW0005         |
+--------------------+
only showing top 2 rows

>>> recordsDF.select("STATION").show(2)
+--------------------+
| STATION            |
+--------------------+
|US1MISW0005         |
|US1MISW0005         |
+--------------------+
only showing top 2 rows

>>> recordsDF.select("STATION", recordsDF.OBSERVATION,
concat("STATION", lit(" - "), recordsDF.OBSERVATION)).show(2)
+------------+------------+-------------------------------------+
| STATION    |OBSERVATION |concat(STATION, - , OBSERVATION)     |
+------------+------------+-------------------------------------+
|US1MISW0005 | PRCP       | US1MISW0005 - PRCP                  |
|US1MISW0005 | SNOW       | US1MISW0005 - SNOW                  |
+------------+------------+-------------------------------------+
only showing top 2 rows
```

It looks familiar, doesn't it? We are using a well-known functionality from relational databases in the form of the function *select()* and some parameters and expressions to obtain the desired behavior. Let's explore some other examples:

```
>>> recordsDF.select("STATION", concat(lit("Observation type: "),
recordsDF.OBSERVATION)).show(2, False)
+--------------+-------------------------------------------+
|STATION       |concat(Observation type: , OBSERVATION)    |
+--------------+-------------------------------------------+
|US1MISW0005   |Observation type: PRCP                     |
|US1MISW0005   |Observation type: SNOW                     |
+--------------+-------------------------------------------+
only showing top 2 rows

>>> recordsDF.select(col("VALUE")+100).show(2)
+----------------+
|(VALUE + 100)   |
+----------------+
|  100           |
|  340           |
+----------------+
only showing top 3 rows
```

In the case of *catalyst expressions*, the DataFrames don't store a value; instead, they store an expression. So for example, let's check the column SOURCE from our DataFrame:

```
>>> recordsDF.select(col("VALUE")).printSchema()
root
     |-- VALUE: integer (nullable = true)
```

It is an *IntegerType()*, but in this case, Spark doesn't store an Integer value; it stores an expression that generates an Integer value from the data. Let's change the type with an expression:

```
>>> recordsDF.select(col("VALUE")).printSchema()
root
 |-- VALUE: integer (nullable = true)

>>> recordsDF.withColumn("VALUE",
col("VALUE").cast("double")).select("VALUE").show(4)
+----------+
|VALUE     |
+----------+
|  0.0     |
|  0.0     |
|  0.0     |
|  401.0   |
+----------+
only showing top 4 rows
```

As you can see, we used *withColumn()* and *cast()* to change the type of a column. Let's name a column with the function *withColumnRenamed()*:

```
>>> recordsDF.withColumn("VALUE",
col("VALUE").cast("double")).select("VALUE").select("VALUE").withCo
lumnRenamed("VALUE", "Value").printSchema()
root
 |-- Value: double (nullable = true)

>>> recordsDF.withColumn("VALUE",
col("VALUE").cast("double")).select("VALUE").select("VALUE").withCo
lumnRenamed("VALUE", "Value").show(4)
+---------+
|Value    |
+---------+
| 0.0     |
| 0.0     |
| 0.0     |
| 401.0   |
+---------+
only showing top 4 rows
```

To copy a column, we can use *withColumn()* again. For example:

```
>>> recordsDF.select("STATION", "OBSERVATION",
"VALUE").withColumn("NewColumn", col("VALUE")).show(4)
+-----------+-----------+------+---------+
| STATION   |OBSERVATION|VALUE |NewColumn|
+-----------+-----------+------+---------+
|US1MISW0005| PRCP      | 0    | 0       |
|US1MISW0005| SNOW      | 0    | 0       |
|CA1MB000296| PRCP      | 0    | 0       |
|ASN00015643| TMAX      | 401  | 401     |
+-----------+-----------+------+---------+
only showing top 4 rows

>>> recordsDF.select("STATION").withColumn("STATION",
concat(lit("Station ID: "), col("STATION"))).show(1, False)
+----------------------+
|STATION               |
+----------------------+
|Station ID: US1MISW0005|
+----------------------+
only showing top 1 row
```

[Continues in next page]

```
>>> recordsDF.printSchema()
root
    |-- STATION: string (nullable = true)
    |-- DATE: integer (nullable = true)
    |-- OBSERVATION: string (nullable = true)
    |-- VALUE: integer (nullable = true)
    |-- MF: string (nullable = true)
    |-- QF: string (nullable = true)
    |-- SF: string (nullable = true)
    |-- TIME: integer (nullable = true)

>>> recordsDF.drop("MF", "QF", "SF").printSchema()
root
    |-- STATION: string (nullable = true)
    |-- DATE: integer (nullable = true)
    |-- OBSERVATION: string (nullable = true)
    |-- VALUE: integer (nullable = true)
    |-- TIME: integer (nullable = true)
```

In the first example, we simply copied the contents of the column SOURCE to NewColumn, and in the second example, we concatenated a literal value in the column NAME, which can be thought of as a replace of the column's contents. And finally, if we want to remove columns from a DataFrame, we use the function *drop()*.

User-Defined Functions

In Spark, you can define your own functions to apply custom actions over columns. They allow you to extend the functionality.

You have to create or define your function and then register it as UDF in order to be able to use it. Let's create an example:

```
>>> from pyspark.sql.types import StructType, ArrayType, LongType,
StringType , IntegerType

>>> from pyspark.sql.functions import udf

>>> records_no_flags = recordsDF.drop("MF", "QF", "SF")

>>> records_no_flags.show(2)
+------------+---------+-----------+------+-----+
| STATION    | DATE    |OBSERVATION |VALUE |TIME |
+------------+---------+-----------+------+-----+
|US1MISW0005 |20180101| PRCP        | 0    |null |
|US1MISW0005 |20180101| SNOW        | 0    |null |
+------------+---------+-----------+------+-----+
only showing top 2 rows
```

[Continues in next page]

```
>>> def fixNullTime(observationTime):
            newTime = observationTime
            if observationTime is None:
                    newTime = 0
            return newTime

>>> udfFixNull=udf(fixNullTime, IntegerType())

>>> records_no_flags.withColumn("TIME",
udfFixNull(col("TIME"))).show(2, False)
+------------+----------+-------------+------+------+
|STATION     |DATE      |OBSERVATION  |VALUE |TIME  |
+------------+----------+-------------+------+------+
|US1MISW0005 |20180101  |PRCP         |0     |0     |
|US1MISW0005 |20180101  |SNOW         |0     |0     |
+------------+----------+-------------+------+------+
only showing top 2 rows
```

In this example, we created a simple function to change Null values to 0, called *fixNullTime(name)*. Using the function *udf()*, the function was registered with Spark, and then using *withColumn()*, the column TIME of the DataFrame *records_no_flags* was replaced by the new value.

7 Spark SQL

DSL stands for Domain Specific Language, and in simple words, it is a language designed for a specific purpose. In the Spark domain, DSL is a language that exposes rich functionality to manipulate data in an SQL-like way; it is SQL for DataFrames. Let's check some examples:

```
>>> from pyspark.sql.functions import col, lit, concat

>>> recordsDF=spark.read.csv('/tmp/2018.csv',inferSchema=True,
header=True)

>>> recordsDF.select("STATION", "OBSERVATION").count()
34126531

>>> recordsDF.select("STATION", "OBSERVATION").distinct().count()
160334

>>> recordsDF.select("STATION", "OBSERVATION").distinct().show(2)
+---------------+------------+
| STATION       |OBSERVATION|
+---------------+------------+
|RP000982230    | TMIN       |
|CA004018642    | TMIN       |
+---------------+------------+

>>> recordsDF.select("STATION",
"OBSERVATION").distinct().limit(2).show()
+---------------+------------+
| STATION       |OBSERVATION|
+---------------+------------+
|RP000982230    | TMIN       |
|CA004018642    | TMIN       |
+---------------+------------+

>>> recordsDF.select("STATION", "OBSERVATION").distinct().count()
160334

>>> recordsDF.select("STATION",
"OBSERVATION").distinct().where(col("STATION")!=
"RP000982230").count()
160330
```

In the examples, *show()* is used to tell Spark to print the contents of the DataFrame.

It by default shows only 20 rows, but if we pass the number of rows as a parameter we can control how many rows it is going to show. For example, *show(2)* is going to print only two rows of data. If you have worked with SQL, maybe some of the statements will look familiar to you. *Select()* allows you to specify which columns you want to show from the DataFrame. *Distinct()* is going to select only different values; it is similar to execute in SQL "SELECT DISTINCT <COLUMN> FROM <TABLE>". *Limit()* comes from MySQL and it is going to limit the amount of data that we are going to select. (In SQL Server, it is called *top*.) For example, *show(2)* is equal in terms of data returned to *limit(2).show()*. And finally, we have *where()*, which allows you to specify conditions when selecting rows. If you remember, we accomplish this task in RDDs by using *filter()*. You can specify several conditions in the *where()* statement by specifying | for OR condition or & for AND condition. Now to sort data, we can use:

```
>>> from pyspark.sql.functions import asc, desc

>>> recordsDF.select("STATION", concat(lit("Observation: "),
"OBSERVATION")).distinct().show(1, False)
+----------------+-------------------------------------------+
|STATION         |concat(Observation: , OBSERVATION)         |
+----------------+-------------------------------------------+
|US1CAAL0004     |Observation: SNOW                          |
+----------------+-------------------------------------------+

>>> recordsDF.select("STATION",
"OBSERVATION").distinct().orderBy("STATION").show(2, False)
+----------------+-----------------+
|STATION         |OBSERVATION      |
+----------------+-----------------+
|AE000041196     |TAVG             |
|AE000041196     |TMIN             |
+----------------+-----------------+

>>> recordsDF.select("STATION",
"OBSERVATION").distinct().orderBy("STATION",
ascending=False).show(2, False)
+----------------+-----------------+
|STATION         |OBSERVATION      |
+----------------+-----------------+
|ZI000067983     |TAVG             |
|ZI000067983     |TMIN             |
+----------------+-----------------+
```

[Continues in next page]

```
>>> recordsDF.select("STATION",
"OBSERVATION").distinct().sort("STATION", ascending=False).show(2,
False)
+--------------------+--------------------+
|STATION             |OBSERVATION         |
+--------------------+--------------------+
|ZI000067983         |TAVG                |
|ZI000067983         |TMIN                |
+--------------------+--------------------+

>>> recordsDF.select("STATION","OBSERVATION").distinct().orderBy(
desc("STATION"), asc("OBSERVATION")).show(2, False)
+--------------------+--------------------+
|STATION             |OBSERVATION         |
+--------------------+--------------------+
|ZI000067983         |PRCP                |
|ZI000067983         |TAVG                |
+--------------------+--------------------+
```

There are two functions to sort data. The first one is *orderBy()*, and like in SQL, you can specify the column you want to use to sort your data. By default it is ascending, but also you can specify *ascending=False* to specify a descending order. By using the functions *desc()* and *asc()* inside *orderBy()*, it is possible to sort your data using two or more rows. The second function you can use is *sort()*, and it is similar to *orderBy()*; you specify the column name,and if you want your data in descending order, just specify the parameter *ascending=False*.

Handling Nulls and Corrupt Data

There is a chance that your data has some corrupt rows or some *null* field values that can affect the queries you want to perform. You can take several actions like removing the rows, filling the null values with a specific value or replacing them. For example:

```
>>> from pyspark.sql.types import StringType

>>> from pyspark.sql.functions import col

>>> recordsDF=spark.read.csv('/tmp/2018.csv',inferSchema=True,
header=True)

>>> recordsDF.count()
34126531

>>> recordsDF.dropna(subset='TIME').count()
8486139
```

[Continues in next page]

```
>>> recordsDF.select("STATION", "OBSERVATION", "TIME").show(2,
False)
+---------------+---------------+--------+
|STATION        |OBSERVATION    |TIME    |
+---------------+---------------+--------+
|US1MISW0005    |PRCP           |null    |
|US1MISW0005    |SNOW           |null    |
+---------------+---------------+--------+

>>> recordsDF.select("STATION", "OBSERVATION",
"TIME").dropna(subset='TIME').show(2, False)
+---------------+---------------+--------+
|STATION        |OBSERVATION    |TIME    |
+---------------+---------------+--------+
|USW00024229    |TMAX           |2400    |
|USW00024229    |TMIN           |2400    |
+---------------+---------------+--------+

>>> recordsDF.select("STATION", "OBSERVATION",
"TIME").fillna(666).show(2, False)
+---------------+---------------+--------+
|STATION        |OBSERVATION    |TIME    |
+---------------+---------------+--------+
|US1MISW0005    |PRCP           |666     |
|US1MISW0005    |SNOW           |666     |
+---------------+---------------+--------+
```

Dropna() receives the following parameters: *how='any'|'all'*. If you use *all*, it is going to delete the row if all columns are null. If you use *any*, it deletes the row if any of the columns are null. Another parameter you can use is *thresh=<int>*. It deletes the row if the row has less than the thresh non-null values. And finally, subset(*'list of columns'*) deletes the rows if in any of the columns specified there is a null value. *Fillna(value)* replaces all null values by *value*.

There are situations where you can have corrupt records, you can separate bad data, drop malformed records or raise an exception, and for this purpose, you can specify the following options when reading information:

```
>>> recordsDF=spark.read.csv('/tmp/2018.csv',inferSchema=True,
header=True, mode='PERMISSIVE',
columnNameOfCorruptRecord='Invalid')

>>> recordsDF=spark.read.csv('/tmp/2018.csv',inferSchema=True,
header=True, mode='DROPMALFORMED')

>>> recordsDF=spark.read.csv('/tmp/2018.csv',inferSchema=True,
header=True, mode='FAILFAST')
```

If you specify *mode='PERMISSIVE',* if it finds a corrupt record, it will add an entry in the column named *'Invalid'.* If you specify *mode='DROPMALFORMED',* Spark will remove all corrupt records, and if *mode='FAILFAST'* is specified, Spark rises an exception.

Saving DataFrames

To save DataFrames, you have to use *DataFrameWriter.* You can use it by using the function *write().* The default format for *write()* is Parquet, but there are many other formats available. For example:

```
>>> recordsDF=spark.read.csv('/tmp/2018.csv',inferSchema=True,
header=True)

>>> recordsDF.write.mode('overwrite').save('/tmp/2018-DF.parquet')

>>> recordsDF.select("STATION").distinct().write.mode('overwrite').
format('text')
        .save('/tmp/2018-Stations.txt')

>>> recordsDF.select("STATION",
"OBSERVATION").distinct().write.mode('overwrite').format('csv').sav
e('/tmp/2018-Stations.csv')
```

When writing, you can specify the *mode().* The options available are *append, overwrite, error* and *ignore.* You can use *option()* or *options()* to control the options of the write format that you selected by specifying *format().*

Spark SQL

It is possible to execute SQL queries in Spark. For this purpose, you use *spark.sql()* and provide the query. To be able to run the queries, you have to create a *view* of your DataFrame. For this purpose, you have to use *createOrReplaceTempView().* Once the view is created, you can run your SQL queries, and the results are returned as a DataFrame.

It is important to mention that Spark SQL is compatible with SQL 2003; Spark has a native SQL parser, and it has subquery support. Let's review some examples:

```
>>> recordsDF=spark.read.csv('/tmp/2018.csv',inferSchema=True,
header=True)

>>> stationsDF=spark.read.csv('/tmp/ghcnd-
stations.csv',inferSchema=True, header=True)

>>> recordsDF.createOrReplaceTempView("RECORDS")

                    [Continues in next page]
```

```
>>> stationsDF.createOrReplaceTempView("STATIONS")

>>> spark.sql('SELECT COUNT(*) FROM RECORDS').show()
+----------------+
|count(1)        |
+----------------+
|34126531        |
+----------------+

>>> spark.sql('SELECT COUNT(*) AS TOTALROWS FROM RECORDS').show()
+----------------+
|TOTALROWS       |
+----------------+
|34126531        |
+----------------+

>>> spark.sql('SELECT DISTINCT STATION, OBSERVATION FROM RECORDS
LIMIT 1').show()
+------------------------+------------------------+
| STATION                |OBSERVATION             |
+------------------------+------------------------+
|RP000982230             | TMIN                   |
+------------------------+------------------------+

>>> spark.sql("SELECT DISTINCT R.STATION, S.STATION_NAME,
R.OBSERVATION FROM RECORDS AS R INNER JOIN STATIONS AS S ON
R.STATION = S.STATION LIMIT 1").show()
+-------------+--------------+----------------+
| STATION     |STATION_NAME  |OBSERVATION     |
+-------------+--------------+----------------+
|USC00426568  | UT OURAY 4NE | PRCP           |
+-------------+--------------+----------------+

>>> spark.sql("SELECT DISTINCT S.STATION_NAME, R.STATION,
R.OBSERVATION FROM RECORDS AS R INNER JOIN STATIONS AS S ON
R.STATION = S.STATION ORDER BY S.STATION_NAME").show(1, False)
+----------------------+-----------------+---------------+
| STATION              |STATION_NAME     |OBSERVATION    |
+----------------------+-----------------+---------------+
| "HOME" MONOGORILBY   |ASN00040708      |PRCP           |
+----------------------+-----------------+---------------+

>>> spark.sql("SELECT DISTINCT S.STATION_NAME, R.STATION,
R.OBSERVATION FROM RECORDS AS R INNER JOIN STATIONS AS S ON
R.STATION = S.STATION ORDER BY S.STATION_NAME DESC").show(1, False)
+---------------+--------------+---------------+
| STATION       |STATION_NAME  |OBSERVATION    |
+---------------+--------------+---------------+
| ZYRJANKA      |RSM00025400   |TMIN           |
+---------------+--------------+---------------+
```

As you can see, Spark SQL is easy and powerful to use. Spark SQL can directly read information from Parquet files. For example:

```
>>> recordsDF=spark.sql("SELECT DISTINCT STATION FROM
PARQUET.`/tmp/2018-DF.parquet/`")

>>> recordsDF2.count()
39598

>>> spark.sql("SELECT DISTINCT STATION FROM PARQUET.`/tmp/2018-
DF.parquet/` ORDER BY STATION DESC LIMIT 1").show()
+-----------------+
|  STATION        |
+-----------------+
|ZI000067983      |
+-----------------+
```

There is more functionality we can use. For example, aggregations:

```
>>> import pyspark.sql.functions as func

>>> recordsDF.groupBy("STATION").count().orderBy("count",
ascending=False).show(2)
+--------------+--------+
|  STATION     |count   |
+--------------+--------+
|USC00218450   | 7985   |
|USC00286055   | 6034   |
+--------------+--------+

>>>
recordsDF.groupBy("STATION").agg(func.count("OBSERVATION")).show(2
+--------------+-------------------+
|  STATION     |count(OBSERVATION) |
+--------------+-------------------+
|USC00340027   | 1821              |
|FIE00145157   | 395               |
+--------------+-------------------+

>>>
recordsDF.groupBy("STATION").agg(func.count("OBSERVATION")).sort(
'count(OBSERVATION)').show(2)
+--------------+-------------------+
|  STATION     |count(OBSERVATION) |
+--------------+-------------------+
|US1SDST0003   | 1                 |
|US10thom004   | 1                 |
+--------------+-------------------+

>>> spark.sql("SELECT STATION, count(*) AS COUNT FROM RECORDS GROUP
BY STATION ORDER BY COUNT DESC").show(2)
+--------------+--------+
|  STATION     |count   |
+--------------+--------+
|USC00218450   | 7985   |
|USC00286055   | 6034   |
+--------------+--------+
```

8 Understanding Typed API: DataSet

In the previous two chapters, we have been using DataFrames. A DataFrame is a special case of Dataset, namely DataSet of Rows. Since Spark 2, we have DataSets as typed API and DataFrames as untyped API. We haven't used Datasets because they are only supported in Scala.

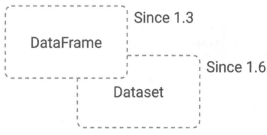

Figure 31: DataFrame and DataSet

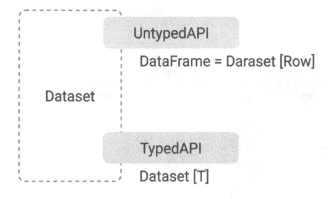

Figure 32: DataSet and DataFrame APIs were unified in Spark 2

Scala is a general purpose programming language. It appeared for the first time in 2004, and it was developed and designed by Martin Odersky. It supports functional programming as well as object-oriented programming. It was designed to address some of the major criticism of Java. It is statically typed, and a cool thing is that it provides interoperability with Java, meaning that it can use Java Libraries, thus greatly increasing the amount of functionality available. An important note is that Spark is written in Scala. It was the first supported language, and it is preferred by the community when working with Spark. For this reason, there are a lot of examples and a large code base of Spark written in Scala

What is a DataSet? Well, it is a collection of strongly typed objects; the collection is distributed, and it is resilient. A DataSet, internally, is implemented using RDDs. It has a schema, and it ensures that you get typed columns, which means all the transformations are typed. Therefore, you are able to detect errors at compile time, which is extremely useful. In order to define a DataSet, you have to first define a Case Class in Scala or use primitive types. A Case Class is just a class that is good for modeling immutable data. DataSet in detail is out of the scope of this book, but let's create an example:

```
scala> val stationsDF = spark.read.option("header",
"true").option("inferSchema", "true").csv("/tmp/ghcnd-
stations.csv")
stationsDF: org.apache.spark.sql.DataFrame = [STATION: string,
LATITUDE: double ... 3 more fields]

scala> stationsDF.printSchema
root
     |-- STATION: string (nullable = true)
     |-- LATITUDE: double (nullable = true)
     |-- LONGITUDE: double (nullable = true)
     |-- ELEVATION: double (nullable = true)

scala> case class Station(id: String, name: String, latitude:
Double, longitude: Double, elevation: Double)
defined class Station

scala> val dataSet = stationsDF.map(row =>
Station(row.getAs[String]("STATION"),
row.getAs[String]("STATION_NAME"), row.getAs[Double]("LATITUDE"),
row.getAs[Double]("LONGITUDE"), row.getAs[Double]("ELEVATION")))
dataSet: org.apache.spark.sql.Dataset[Station] = [id: string, name:
string ... 3 more fields]
```

[Continues in next page]

```
scala> dataSet.show(2)
+-----------+--------------------+--------+---------+---------+
| id        | name               |latitude|longitude|elevation |
+-----------+--------------------+--------+---------+---------+
|ACW00011604| ST JOHNS COOLIDG...| 17.1167| -61.7833| 10.1    |
|ACW00011647| ST JOHNS          | 17.1333| -61.7833| 19.2    |
+-----------+--------------------+--------+---------+---------+
only showing top 2 rows

scala> dataSet.count
res5: Long = 108081
```

In the example, we used the word *val* to declare an immutable variable, and the data was loaded into the variable *stationsDF*. We have available all the functions we have studied in previous chapters. For example, we used *show(), orderBy()* and *printSchema.*

Xavier Morera & Nereo Campos

9 Spark Streaming

Spark Streaming is an extension of Spark API. It performs streaming analytics in a scalable, high-throughput and fault-tolerant fashion. Data can be obtained from several sources, for example, messaging queue systems like Apache Kafka or AWS Kinesis, and services for collecting, aggregating and moving large amounts of data like Apache Flume or simple TCP sockets.

Spark streaming works as follows:

- Live input data is received by Spark as a stream.
- Data is divided into batches.
- Batches are processed by Spark Engine.
- Batches of results of processed data are generated as a stream of results.

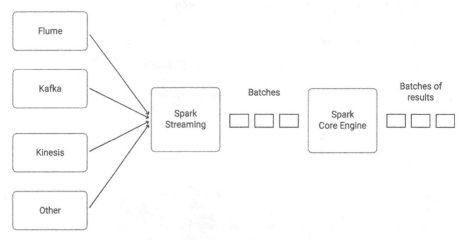

Figure 33:Spark Streaming

Batches of results of processed data can be ingested into file systems, databases and live dashboards.

One of the key concepts of Spark Streaming is the high-level abstraction called Discretized Stream, or DStream. Spark Streaming is a continuous sequence of RDDs of the same type that represent the input streaming data. When a transformation like *map()* is applied to a DStream, a new DStream is created. Spark core doesn't know it is processing a stream of live data; Spark streaming is receiving, creating, transforming and coordinating the streaming of data as DStream that is going to be consumed by Spark Core as RDDs. Let's check an example:

```
>>> sc.stop()

>>> from pyspark import SparkContext

>>> from pyspark.streaming import StreamingContext

>>> sc = SparkContext("local[2]", "ObservationTypesCount")

>>> ssc = StreamingContext(sc, 1)

>>> stream_records = ssc.socketTextStream("localhost", 18667)

>>> events = stream_records.map(lambda record:
record.split(",")[2])

>>> events_map = events.map(lambda event: (event, 1))

>>> events_count = events_map.reduceByKey(lambda x, y: x + y)

>>> events_count.pprint()

>>> ssc.start()

>>> ssc.awaitTermination()
------------------- Time: 2019-04-11 14:25:17 -------------------
------------------- Time: 2019-04-11 14:25:18 -------------------
------------------- Time: 2019-04-11 14:26:33 -------------------
(u'TMAX', 3)
(u'TMIN', 2)
(u'PRCP', 6)
(u'SNOW', 3)
------------------- Time: 2019-04-11 14:28:37 -------------------
(u'SNWD', 3)
(u'PRCP', 7)
(u'SNOW', 3)
------------------- Time: 2019-04-11 14:28:42 -------------------
------------------- Time: 2019-04-11 14:28:43 -------------------
------------------- Time: 2019-04-11 14:28:44 -------------------
------------------- Time: 2019-04-11 14:28:45 -------------------
```

Let me explain how it works:

- Spark context is stopped and recreated to set the name of our application.
- Using *StreamingContext*, an entry point for our streaming application is created.
- A *socketTextStream* is used to define that we are going to receive a stream of data from an application publishing in the local host in the port 18,667.
- The application is expecting to receive lines from our RECORDS dataset, for example `US1MISW0005,20180101,PRCP,0,,,N,`
- The creation of the batches from the stream happens behind the scenes, and we don't have control over it.
- A *map()* to split each line by ',' and extract the event type is applied to the stream of data.
- Then another *map()* is used to create pairs in the form *(EventType, 1)*.
- Using *reduceByKey()*, the application counts the number of events of each type we are receiving in each batch from the stream.
- *Pprint()* is used to print the results.
- *Ssc.start()* is used to start our application; in that moment, we see prints in the console starting with "------------------------------ *Time:*". This means our Spark streaming application is waiting to receive data.

The application sending streaming data is just sending a small number of records from the RECORDS dataset; in the first attempt, it sent the following records:

```
US1MISW0005,20180101,PRCP,0,,,N,
US1MISW0005,20180101,SNOW,0,,,N,
CA1MB000296,20180101,PRCP,0,,,N,
ASN00015643,20180101,TMAX,401,,,a,
ASN00015643,20180101,TMIN,234,,,a,
ASN00015643,20180101,PRCP,0,,,a,
US1LAEB0041,20180101,PRCP,0,,,N,
US1LAEB0041,20180101,SNOW,0,,,N,
ASN00085296,20180101,TMAX,253,,,a,
ASN00085296,20180101,TMIN,125,,,a,
ASN00085296,20180101,PRCP,0,,,a,
US1KSSG0097,20180101,PRCP,0,,,N,
US1KSSG0097,20180101,SNOW,0,,,N,
ASN00085280,20180101,TMAX,262,,,a,
ASN00085280,20180101,TMIN,155,,,a,
```

By inspecting the records, we can verify that Spark reported the right values of counts of Event Type, in this case *(u'TMAX', 3) (u'TMIN', 2) (u'PRCP', 6) (u'SNOW', 3)*. The second attempt the application sent is:

```
ASN00085280,20180101,PRCP,2,,,a,
ASN00040209,20180101,PRCP,0,,,a,
US1KSEL0074,20180101,PRCP,0,,,N,
US1INNW0001,20180101,PRCP,0,,,N,
US1INNW0001,20180101,SNOW,0,,,N,
US1INNW0001,20180101,SNWD,127,,,N,
US1INKS0032,20180101,PRCP,0,T,,N,
US1INKS0032,20180101,SNOW,0,T,,N,
US1INKS0032,20180101,SNWD,127,,,N,
US1INFL0003,20180101,PRCP,3,,,N,
US1INFL0003,20180101,SNOW,3,,,N,
US1INFL0003,20180101,SNWD,127,,,N,
US1ILMG0006.20180101.PRCP.0...N.
```

The second time, the result was *(u'SNWD', 3) (u'PRCP', 7) (u'SNOW', 3)*. As we can see, using Spark Streaming is as simple as using Spark.

10 Exploring NOOA's Datasets

We have learned about Spark Core, DataFrames, Spark SQL, DataSets and Spark Streaming. We have showed most of the features available in Spark by using two datasets, one called RECORDS that contains all the metrics collected by weather stations around the world during 2018 and another one called STATIONS that contains information related to the stations that collected all the information like latitude, longitude and elevation. If you take a look in NOOA's website, namely in **https://www1.ncdc.noaa.gov/pub/data/ghcn/daily/by_year/**, there is data from 1763 to the present. Exploring the datasets, you can find that during the last 250 years some monitoring stations have been removed and new ones have been added. Also, you may find that there are multiple types of observations (for example, TMIN, DATX, TMAX, SNOW and PRCP) and some of them have been added in recent years, and finally not all the stations collect all the information.

In this chapter, we will use our knowledge from previous chapters to explore the datasets from NOOA, starting with checking how some observation types have changed between 1918 and 2018; later we will load and explore more data to compare our findings.

To start this exercise, let's load our datasets and explore some basic functionalities that can give us a lot of information:

```
>>> from pyspark.sql.functions import *

>>> records_2018=spark.read.csv('/tmp/2018.csv',inferSchema=True,
header=True)

>>> records_1918=spark.read.csv('/tmp/1918.csv',inferSchema=True,
header=True) >>> stations=spark.read.csv('/tmp/ghcnd-
stations.csv',inferSchema=True, header=True)

>>> records_2018.count()
34126531

>>> records_1918.count()
9509887

>>> stations.count()
108081
```

Our first insights are that we have three datasets: records for 2018 are 34 million, records for 1918 are 9 million, and we have 108,081 stations. Those stations include all the stations since 1763. Let's check the schema inferred by Spark:

```
>>> stations.printSchema()
root
    |-- STATION: string (nullable = true)
    |-- LATITUDE: double (nullable = true)
    |-- LONGITUDE: double (nullable = true)
    |-- ELEVATION: double (nullable = true)
    |-- STATION_NAME: string (nullable = true)

>>> records_2018.printSchema()
root
    |-- STATION: string (nullable = true)
    |-- DATE: integer (nullable = true)
    |-- OBSERVATION: string (nullable = true)
    |-- VALUE: integer (nullable = true)
    |-- MF: string (nullable = true)
    |-- QF: string (nullable = true)
    |-- SF: string (nullable = true)
    |-- TIME: integer (nullable = true)

>>> records_1918.printSchema()
root
    |-- STATION: string (nullable = true)
    |-- DATE: integer (nullable = true)
    |-- OBSERVATION: string (nullable = true)
    |-- VALUE: integer (nullable = true)
    |-- MF: string (nullable = true)
    |-- QF: string (nullable = true)
    |-- SF: string (nullable = true)
    |-- TIME: integer (nullable = true)
```

The schemas of the datasets for 2018 and 1918 are equal; that's important because the format of our data is equal. This simplifies the analysis. Let's review how many stations and observations are used in each dataset:

```
>>> records_2018.select("STATION").distinct().count()
39598

>>> records_2018.select("OBSERVATION").distinct().count()
68

>>> records_1918.select("STATION").distinct().count()
13818

>>> records_1918.select("OBSERVATION").distinct().count()
31
```

For 2018, there were 39,598 stations collecting data actively. For 1918, there were only 13,818 stations. On the other hand, there are 68 types of observation in the 2018 dataset, and only 31 for 1918. Now let's check which stations were active in 1918 and which are active nowadays.

```
>>>stations_1918=records_1918.select(col("STATION").alias("STATION_
1918")).distinct()

>>>stations_2018=records_2018.select(col("STATION").alias("STATION_
2018")).distinct()

>>> stations_2018.join(stations_1918, col("STATION_1918") ==
col("STATION_2018")).count()
3482
```

There are only 3,482 stations active now that were active 100 years ago. We are going to focus our exploration on those stations because we want to compare data from 2018 with data from 1918. Let's add those 3,482 stations in a DataFrame and use it to filter data from 2018 and 1918.

```
>>> stations_100_years=stations_1918.join(stations_2018,
stations_1918["STATION_1918"]==stations_2018["STATION_2018"]).selec
t(col("STATION_2018").alias("STATION_100_YEARS"))

>>> stations_100_years.count()
3482

>>> records_100_years_1918=stations_100_years.join(records_1918,
col("STATION") == col("STATION_100_YEARS")).select([col(colname)
for colname in records_1918.columns])

>>> records_100_years_2018=stations_100_years.join(records_2018,
col("STATION") == col("STATION_100_YEARS")).select([col(colname)
for colname in records_2018.columns])

>>> records_100_years_1918.count()
3057279

>>> records_100_years_2018.count()
4005275
```

There are 3,057,279 records corresponding to the 3,482 stations active since 1918 in the dataset for 1918, and 4,005,275 for the year 2018. Now that we have several transformations to obtain exactly the records we need to compare the year 2018 with 1918, we have to make a decision; we can use *cache()* and *unpersist()* to manage the memory and the lineage and avoid having Spark recalculate with each action, or we can simply write our data ready to be analyzed to a file and load them later. At this point, we decided to save it to a file:

```
>>> records_100_years_2018.write.parquet("/tmp/records_100_years_
2018.parquet")

>>> records_100_years_1918.write.parquet("/tmp/records_100_years_
1918.parquet")
```

If we recall from previous chapters, an excellent format to store data is *parquet*, for many reasons. It is compressed with optimized storage, so it saves a lot of storage and computation time. Now let's load our data again and continue:

```
>>> records_2018=spark.read.parquet("/tmp/records_100_years_2018
.parquet")

>>> records_1918=spark.read.parquet("/tmp/records_100_years_1918
.parquet")
```

Our data, ready to be analyzed, is back in memory. Let's calculate the average of the value of each observation for each station for years 2018 and 1918:

```
>>> records_2018_avg=records_2018.select(col("STATION"),
col("OBSERVATION"), col("VALUE")).groupBy("STATION",
"OBSERVATION").agg(avg("VALUE").alias("AVG")).orderBy("STATION",
"OBSERVATION")

>>> records_1918_avg=records_1918.select(col("STATION"),
col("OBSERVATION"), col("VALUE")).groupBy("STATION",
"OBSERVATION").agg(avg("VALUE").alias("AVG")).orderBy("STATION",
"OBSERVATION")

>>> records_2018_avg.count()
17957

>>> records_1918_avg.count()
12837

>>> records_2018_avg.show(1, False)
+------------+------------+------------------+
|STATION     |OBSERVATION |AVG               |
+------------+------------+------------------+
|AGE00147716 |PRCP        |11.537537537537538|
+------------+------------+------------------+
only showing top 1 row

>>> records_1918_avg.show(1, False)
+------------+------------+------------------+
|STATION     |OBSERVATION |AVG               |
+------------+------------+------------------+
|AGE00147716 |PRCP        |215.0             |
+------------+------------+------------------+
only showing top 1 row
```

There is an average of 17,957 records for 2018 and 12,837 for 1918. Our data is organized by STATION, OBSERVATION and AVG. We are going to filter these results by the type of observation we want to analyze. Because the most common ones are precipitation, maximum and minimum temperature, all records will be filtered by PRCP, TMAX and TMIN:

```
>>> basic_types_2018=records_2018_avg
    .where(col("OBSERVATION").isin(["PRCP", "TMAX", "TMIN"]))
    .select([col(colname).alias("2018_"+colname) for colname in
records_2018_avg.columns])

>>> basic_types_1918=records_1918_avg
    .where(col("OBSERVATION").isin(["PRCP", "TMAX", "TMIN"]))
    .select([col(colname).alias("1918_"+colname) for colname in
records_1918_avg.columns])
```

It is interesting to show side by side the average for the same STATION and OBSERVATION for the years 2018 and 1918. We can use *join()* for this purpose:

```
>>> data_2018_1918=basic_types_2018.join(basic_types_1918,
(col("2018_STATION") == col("1918_STATION")) &
(col("2018_OBSERVATION") ==
col("1918_OBSERVATION"))).join(stations, col("STATION") ==
col("1918_STATION"))

>>> data_2018_1918.count()
6312

>>> data_2018_1918.printSchema()
root
 |-- 2018_STATION: string (nullable = true)
 |-- 2018_OBSERVATION: string (nullable = true)
 |-- 2018_AVG: double (nullable = true)
 |-- 1918_STATION: string (nullable = true)
 |-- 1918_OBSERVATION: string (nullable = true)
 |-- 1918_AVG: double (nullable = true)
 |-- STATION: string (nullable = true)
 |-- LATITUDE: double (nullable = true)
 |-- LONGITUDE: double (nullable = true)
 |-- ELEVATION: double (nullable = true)
 |-- STATION_NAME: string (nullable = true)

>>> data_2018_1918.select("STATION", "STATION_NAME",
"2018_OBSERVATION", "2018_AVG", "1918_AVG").show(2, False)
+-----------+---------+---------+---------+---------+
|STA...     |STA_NAME |2018_OBS |2018_AVG |1918_AVG |
+-----------+---------+---------+---------+---------+
|AGE00147716| NEMOURS |PRCP     |11.53    |215.0    |
|AGE00147716| NEMOURS |TMAX     |225.44   |150.0    |
+-----------+---------+---------+---------+---------+
```

As we can see by printing the schema, columns from 2018 and 1918 datasets were joined, and then the result was joined to the station dataset. We have our data ready; it is time to save it to avoid having to recalculate everything. After saving it, we are going to load it:

```
>>> data_2018_1918.select("STATION",
col("2018_OBSERVATION").alias("OBSERVATION"), "2018_AVG",
"1918_AVG", "LATITUDE", "LONGITUDE", "ELEVATION",
"STATION_NAME").write.parquet("/tmp/data_2018_1918.parquet")

>>>
data_2018_1918=spark.read.parquet("/tmp/data_2018_1918.parquet")
```

Let's calculate the difference between the average for each type of observation for each station between 2018 and 1918 and order the results by the observations and stations that have a bigger difference:

```
>>> data_2018_1918.select("STATION", "STATION_NAME", "LATITUDE",
"LONGITUDE", "ELEVATION","OBSERVATION", (abs(col("2018_AVG")-
col("1918_AVG"))).alias("DIFFABS"),(col("2018_AVG")-
col("1918_AVG")).alias("DIFF"), "2018_AVG",
"1918_AVG").orderBy(desc("DIFFABS")).show(2, False)
+-----------+-----------------+---------+----------+----------+
----------+------------------+------------------+----------+--
---------------+
|STATION    |STATION_NAME
|LATITUDE|LONGITUDE|ELEVATION|OBSERVATION      |DIFFABS
|DIFF             |2018_AVG         |1918_AVG          |
+-----------+-----------------+---------+----------+----------+
----------+------------------+------------------+----------+--
---------------+
|ASN00039040|GIN POST OFFICE|-24.9933|151.9606 |64.0       |PRCP
|855.7534246575342|855.7534246575342|880.0              |24.2465753
42465754|
|RSM00024266|VERHOJANSK       |67.5667 |133.4     |136.0      |TMAX
|437.5150265585686|437.5150265585686|-22.291095890410958|-
459.8061224489796|
+-----------+-----------------+---------+----------+----------+
----------+------------------+------------------+----------+--
---------------+
only showing top 2 rows
```

FINAL WORDS

AND SO THE BOOK ENDS, BUT NOT YOUR LEARNING JOURNEY. We sincerely hope that this book helped you learn Spark, which opens a whole set of possibilities to work with data, not only as a data engineer, but also as someone who is interested in the exciting world of machine learning.

The world is changing, and remaining at the top of your game can help you create a future for yourself. No one is in charge of your future except you. It is my most humble opinion that you should not rely on your employer to define your career path.

You have only one life to live, so learn new and exciting things. Work on projects that make you passionate, things that keep you up at night and put you in a bad mood on Friday because the week is ending, and make you happy on Monday because it's time for that special project. That is how I live. But don't forget your family; no professional success can justify a personal failure.

On the other hand, if you like your job and want to work 9 to 5 and forget about it when you clock out, then that is ok as well.

Just remember that what you learn is yours for life.

ABOUT THE AUTHORS

THIS BOOK WAS CREATED AS A COLLABORATION between two good friends and former coworkers, Xavier Morera and Nereo Campos.

Nereo, as you'll hear from anyone who has ever worked with him, is one of those people who makes the hard things look easy—but more than that, he is always willing to sit down and help you with whatever you are stuck on.

He has an impeccable character; he is dependable, always delivers, and is someone you can count on.

Xavier runs his life based on a few premises, but there is one that comes to mind now:

Build your dream before someone else hires you to build theirs.

He has worked as an independent contractor for most of his career. He left a stable job at ArtinSoft (Artificial Intelligence Software) in 2005, where in collaboration with HP, he taught Microsoft partners how to migrate 32-bit applications to 64-bit—he aided with the creation of the migration labs that were delivered all over the world.

Xavier helped create and grow a software development company out of Costa Rica, then moved and became a contractor with Search Technologies (now part of Accenture). There, he was introduced to the wonderful world of enterprise search and Big Data, his current focus.

A few years later, he started creating courses for Pluralsight, **https://www.pluralsight.com/authors/xavier-morera**, and has also helped create courses and develop applications for other companies like Cloudera, of which he is quite a fan.

He loves off roading in his old Land Rover and loves his family. Also, he is always willing to help.

You can find him at **http://www.xaviermorera.com**.